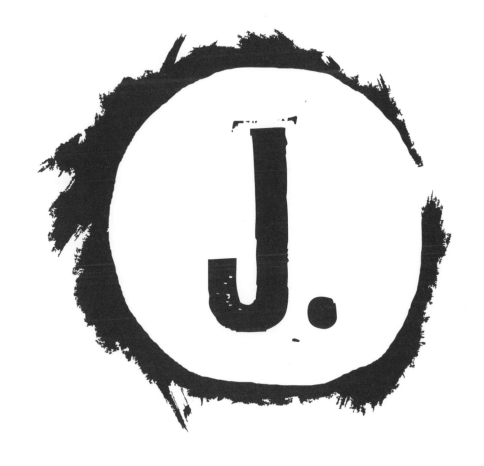

JESUS-CENTERED
Planner
2 0 2 2

DISCOVERING WHO JESUS SAYS I AM EVERY DAY

Jesus-Centered Planner 2022
Discovering Who Jesus Says I Am Every Day

Copyright © 2021 Group Publishing, Inc./0000 0001 0362 4853
Lifetree™ is an imprint of Group Publishing, Inc.
Visit our websites: **MyLifetree.com** and **group.com**

The Jesus-Centered 2022 planner was created for you by the talented team at Group.

Scripture quotations are taken from the *Holy Bible*, New Living Translation, copyright ©1996, 2004, 2015 by Tyndale House Foundation. Used by permission of Tyndale House Publishers, Inc., Carol Stream, Illinois 60188. All rights reserved.

ISBN 978-1-4707-6633-7
Printed in China.

Welcome
to a New Year With Jesus!

Dearly loved Jesus-follower,

As you face a new year, you may wonder, "What will happen?" "Will I ever get what I've always wanted?" "How will I cope with so much change?"

Jesus knows these wonderings—even if you never speak them aloud. And he's inviting you to ask him something else. It's a question whose answer makes all the difference. So perhaps this year it's also time to ask Jesus one of the most important questions you'll ever ask:

"Jesus, who do you say I am?"

Through the pages of this planner, you'll listen for his response. Not just once, but every single day. After you ask, listen. Let Jesus speak to you about who he's created you to be. New. Growing. Free. Friend.

With each new week, you'll find a fresh perspective on your identity in Jesus. Let this identity sink in as you go through each day. The process will leave you encouraged, equipped, and resting in who Jesus says you are.

(This year, as an added catalyst, we've paired the planner's Bible-reading plan and weekly devotional thoughts with the *Namesake: Revealing Who Jesus Says I Am* devotional coloring book.)

2022

January

S	M	T	W	T	F	S
						1
2	3	4	5	6	7	8
9	10	11	12	13	14	15
16	**17**	18	19	20	21	22
23	24	25	26	27	28	29
30	31					

February

S	M	T	W	T	F	S
		1	2	3	4	5
6	7	8	9	10	11	12
13	**14**	15	16	17	18	19
20	**21**	22	23	24	25	26
27	28					

March

S	M	T	W	T	F	S
		1	2	3	4	5
6	7	8	9	10	11	12
13	14	15	16	17	18	19
20	21	22	23	24	25	26
27	28	29	30	31		

April

S	M	T	W	T	F	S
					1	2
3	4	5	6	7	8	9
10	11	12	13	14	**15**	16
17	18	19	20	21	22	23
24	25	26	27	28	29	30

May

S	M	T	W	T	F	S
1	2	3	4	5	6	7
8	9	10	11	12	13	14
15	16	17	18	19	20	21
22	23	24	25	26	27	28
29	**30**	31				

June

S	M	T	W	T	F	S
			1	2	3	4
5	6	7	8	9	10	11
12	13	14	15	16	17	18
19	20	21	22	23	24	25
26	27	28	29	30		

July

S	M	T	W	T	F	S
					1	2
3	**4**	5	6	7	8	9
10	11	12	13	14	15	16
17	18	19	20	21	22	23
24	25	26	27	28	29	30
31						

August

S	M	T	W	T	F	S
	1	2	3	4	5	6
7	8	9	10	11	12	13
14	15	16	17	18	19	20
21	22	23	24	25	26	27
28	29	30	31			

September

S	M	T	W	T	F	S
				1	2	3
4	**5**	6	7	8	9	10
11	12	13	14	15	16	17
18	19	20	21	22	23	24
25	26	27	28	29	30	

October

S	M	T	W	T	F	S
						1
2	3	4	5	6	7	8
9	10	11	12	13	14	15
16	17	18	19	20	21	22
23	24	25	26	27	28	29
30	**31**					

November

S	M	T	W	T	F	S
		1	2	3	4	5
6	7	8	9	10	**11**	12
13	14	15	16	17	18	19
20	21	22	23	**24**	25	26
27	28	29	30			

December

S	M	T	W	T	F	S
				1	2	3
4	5	6	7	8	9	10
11	12	13	14	15	16	17
18	19	20	21	22	23	**24**
25	26	27	28	29	30	**31**

U.S. Holidays

Jan 1	New Year's Day	Apr 17	Easter	Oct 31	Halloween
Jan 17	Martin Luther King Jr. Day	May 8	Mother's Day	Nov 11	Veterans Day
Feb 14	Valentine's Day	May 30	Memorial Day	Nov 24	Thanksgiving Day
Feb 21	Presidents Day	Jun 19	Father's Day	Dec 24	Christmas Eve
Apr 10	Palm Sunday	Jul 4	Independence Day	Dec 25	Christmas Day
Apr 15	Good Friday	Sep 5	Labor Day	Dec 31	New Year's Eve

2023

January

S	M	T	W	T	F	S
1	2	3	4	5	6	7
8	9	10	11	12	13	14
15	**16**	17	18	19	20	21
22	23	24	25	26	27	28
29	30	31				

February

S	M	T	W	T	F	S
			1	2	3	4
5	6	7	8	9	10	11
12	13	**14**	15	16	17	18
19	**20**	21	22	23	24	25
26	27	28				

March

S	M	T	W	T	F	S
			1	2	3	4
5	6	7	8	9	10	11
12	13	14	15	16	17	18
19	20	21	22	23	24	25
26	27	28	29	30	31	

April

S	M	T	W	T	F	S
						1
2	3	4	5	6	**7**	8
9	10	11	12	13	14	15
16	17	18	19	20	21	22
23	24	25	26	27	28	29
30						

May

S	M	T	W	T	F	S
	1	2	3	4	5	6
7	8	9	10	11	12	13
14	15	16	17	18	19	20
21	22	23	24	25	26	27
28	**29**	30	31			

June

S	M	T	W	T	F	S
				1	2	3
4	5	6	7	8	9	10
11	12	13	14	15	16	17
18	19	20	21	22	23	24
25	26	27	28	29	30	

July

S	M	T	W	T	F	S
						1
2	3	**4**	5	6	7	8
9	10	11	12	13	14	15
16	17	18	19	20	21	22
23	24	25	26	27	28	29
30	31					

August

S	M	T	W	T	F	S
		1	2	3	4	5
6	7	8	9	10	11	12
13	14	15	16	17	18	19
20	21	22	23	24	25	26
27	28	29	30	31		

September

S	M	T	W	T	F	S
					1	2
3	**4**	5	6	7	8	9
10	11	12	13	14	15	16
17	18	19	20	21	22	23
24	25	26	27	28	29	30

October

S	M	T	W	T	F	S
1	2	3	4	5	6	7
8	9	10	11	12	13	14
15	16	17	18	19	20	21
22	23	24	25	26	27	28
29	30	**31**				

November

S	M	T	W	T	F	S
			1	2	3	4
5	6	7	8	9	10	**11**
12	13	14	15	16	17	18
19	20	21	22	**23**	24	25
26	27	28	29	30		

December

S	M	T	W	T	F	S
					1	2
3	4	5	6	7	8	9
10	11	12	13	14	15	16
17	18	19	20	21	22	23
24	**25**	26	27	28	29	30
31						

U.S. Holidays

Jan 1	New Year's Day
Jan 16	Martin Luther King Jr. Day
Feb 14	Valentine's Day
Feb 20	Presidents Day
Apr 2	Palm Sunday
Apr 7	Good Friday
Apr 9	Easter Sunday
May 14	Mother's Day
May 29	Memorial Day
Jun 18	Father's Day
Jul 4	Independence Day
Sep 4	Labor Day
Oct 31	Halloween
Nov 11	Veterans Day
Nov 23	Thanksgiving Day
Dec 24	Christmas Eve
Dec 25	Christmas Day
Dec 31	New Year's Eve

How to Use This Planner

The *Jesus-Centered Planner* is designed to help you let Jesus guide the way you organize your life and set your priorities each day, week, month, and quarter. Here's how your planner works.

Establishing Priorities

Priority worksheets allow you to let Jesus help you decide what's most important to focus on in your life for the near future. Our busy lives and constant distractions can keep us from giving our attention to what matters most, so these quarterly priority worksheets give you an opportunity to choose your life's priorities for reasonable periods of time.

> REMINDER: Use a pencil for this section, and limit yourself to a maximum of three priorities.

With Jesus' command in mind, prayerfully consider your top priority—what's the most important investment of your time and energy—for you to focus on for the next three months. Your priority can be anything: your family, job, friends, special project—whichever part of your life you want to be more centered on Jesus.

1ST QUARTER PRIORITY (JANUARY, FEBRUARY, MARCH)

Focusing on this priority is important to *you* because…

Tips for Setting Priorities

Use a pencil. This eliminates the pressure of having to choose the "perfect" priorities and gives you the flexibility to tweak or change them week by week.

Limit yourself to up to three top priorities per quarter. Avoid overwhelming yourself with trying to do too much at a time. The fewer priorities you focus on, the better chance you have of staying committed to those priorities.

Pray about it. Remember, this is a Jesus-centered planner. Talk to Jesus, and listen to his direction.

Monthly Calendar

JANUARY 2022

To Do	Sunday	Monday	Tuesday	Wednesday	Thursday	Friday	Saturday
	26	27	28	29	30	31	1 New Year's Day
	2	3	4	5	6	7	8
	9	10	11	12	13	14	15
Notes	16	17 Martin Luther King Jr. Day	18	19	20	21	22
	23	24	25	26	27	28	29
	30	31	1	2	3	4	5

This month, keep your priorities focused on Jesus by...

Loving others: Loving others must always show up in your priorities. Who are you going to focus on loving this month? Write one to three names here, and schedule time to reach out to those people.

Use your monthly calendar to make sure your priorities align with Jesus' priorities.

This calendar prompts you to identify at least one way to focus on Jesus every month. It also encourages you to follow Jesus' example by focusing on loving others every month.

This month, keep your priorities focused on Jesus by...

Loving others: Loving others must always show up in your priorities. Who are you going to focus on loving this month? Write one to three names here, and schedule time to reach out to those people.

Weekly Schedule

26 Sunday	27 Monday	28 Tuesday	29 Wednesday	30 Thursday	31 Friday	1 Saturday	What are your prayer priorities this week?
						READ *Genesis 1*	
6:00	6:00	6:00	6:00	6:00	6:00	6:00	
7:00	7:00	7:00	7:00	7:00	7:00	7:00	
8:00	8:00	8:00	8:00	8:00	8:00	8:00	
9:00	9:00	9:00	9:00	9:00	9:00	9:00	
10:00	10:00	10:00	10:00	10:00	10:00	10:00	
11:00	11:00	11:00	11:00	11:00	11:00	11:00	
12:00	12:00	12:00	12:00	12:00	12:00	12:00	
1:00	1:00	1:00	1:00	1:00	1:00	1:00	
2:00	2:00	2:00	2:00	2:00	2:00	2:00	
3:00	3:00	3:00	3:00	3:00	3:00	3:00	To Do
4:00	4:00	4:00	4:00	4:00	4:00	4:00	
5:00	5:00	5:00	5:00	5:00	5:00	5:00	
6:00	6:00	6:00	6:00	6:00	6:00	6:00	
7:00	7:00	7:00	7:00	7:00	7:00	7:00	
8:00	8:00	8:00	8:00	8:00	8:00	8:00	
9:00	9:00	9:00	9:00	9:00	9:00	9:00	
10:00	10:00	10:00	10:00	10:00	10:00	10:00	

You bring out the best. Though the world is full of robust flavors, they leave an artificial aftertaste on the tongue. *But not you.* You're salt. Natural and authentic, you bring out the best flavors in those around you. You're my preserving agent, unlocking the true taste of the life you've found in me.

Love, Jesus

Matthew 5:13

Things you're thankful for this week:

The weekly schedule is going to be the primary part of this planner that helps you stay centered on Jesus. These four features are designed to help you keep your vision for the year in focus:

- **Jesus-centered devotional prompt:** Every week you'll find a creative new way to stay connected to Jesus and keep him at your center every day. The devotional prompts and the Bible-reading plan are taken from *Namesake: Revealing Who Jesus Says I Am.* It's a perfect creative and colorful companion for your journey with Jesus.

- **Gratitude prompt:** Record the things you're most grateful for each week, giving thanks to Jesus for each one.

- **Prayer prompt:** Take time to talk with Jesus every week.

- **Jesus-centered daily Bible-reading plan:** Because all of the Bible points to the Messiah, reading the story of God can point you to a deeper relationship with Jesus. This chapter-a-day reading plan includes 365 readings from the 1,189 chapters in the Bible, so it's still just a sampler. But follow this month-by-month plan and you'll have a much deeper grasp of what the whole Bible is all about: the person and work of Jesus Christ. Use the *Jesus-Centered Bible*, which features Jesus connections from Genesis to Revelation, to get the most out of your daily reading time.

You bring out the best. Though the world is full of robust flavors, they leave an artificial aftertaste on the tongue. *But not you.* You're salt. Natural and authentic, you bring out the best flavors in those around you. You're my preserving agent, unlocking the true taste of the life you've found in me.

Love, Jesus

Matthew 5:13

- **Jesus-centered devotional prompt**

Things you're thankful for this week:

- **Gratitude prompt**

- **Prayer prompt**

- **Jesus-centered daily Bible-reading plan**

What are your prayer priorities this week?

WEEK 2
JAN 2 – JAN 8

2 Sunday

READ
Genesis 2

6:00

7:00

8:00

3 Monday

READ
John 1

6:00

7:00

8:00

Monthly Reflections

Review your gratitude notes from previous weeks, and write a prayer to Jesus thanking him for this month.

....

....

....

....

....

....

What experiences, insights, and moments helped keep Jesus a priority in your life in January? Record them here so you don't forget them.

....

....

....

Reviewing the previous month, how did focusing on the right priorities make a difference in your life?

....

....

....

Are there any ways you might adjust your priorities in the month ahead?

....

....

Review your appointments and tasks for the coming month. In what ways are they helping you focus on Jesus' priority of loving others? Is there anything you need to cancel, add, or change? Pray about it; then update your schedule as needed.

Now write a prayer thanking Jesus for new opportunities coming in February, including one way you're planning to stay focused on him.

....

....

....

At the end of each month, you'll have a chance to recall what you've experienced and reflect on how Jesus has impacted your life. Through a series of questions, you'll review your priorities, celebrate accomplishments, and look forward to each new month.

Blank Pages

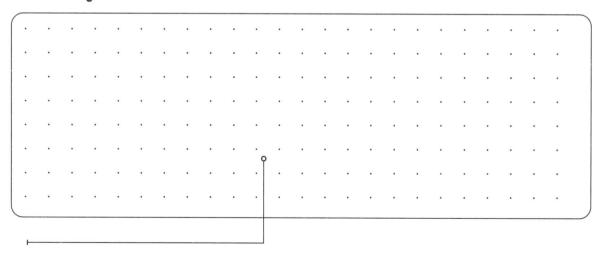

You'll find blank pages at the back of your planner. Use them for lists, tracking projects, journaling, prayers, doodling, budgeting—whatever you like.

What It Means to Be Jesus-Centered

Using a Jesus-centered planner doesn't make you Jesus-centered. Singing songs about Jesus doesn't make you Jesus-centered. Driving around town with an "I love Jesus" bumper sticker doesn't make you Jesus-centered. Even reading your Bible every day doesn't mean your life is centered on Jesus.

So what is being "Jesus-centered" really all about? How do you make Jesus the hub of your life?

Jesus tells us how in John 15: "When you obey my commandments, you remain in my love... This is my commandment: Love each other in the same way I have loved you" (John 15:10, 12).

The key to staying attached to the Vine—to staying centered on Jesus—is to love others. You cannot be Jesus-centered if you aren't actively loving other people.

Loving others is pretty straightforward. First Corinthians 13:4-7 describes it for us: "Love is patient and kind. Love is not jealous or boastful or proud or rude. It does not demand its own way. It is not irritable, and it keeps no record of being wronged. It does not rejoice about injustice but rejoices whenever the truth wins out. Love never gives up, never loses faith, is always hopeful, and endures through every circumstance."

As you use this planner in the weeks and months ahead, remember that perhaps its greatest purpose may be in helping you organize your life around loving other people. If that's all you accomplish in the next year, you will most certainly be living a genuine Jesus-centered life.

Setting Jesus-Centered Priorities, First Quarter

Look to Jesus' example to guide your life's priorities.

Before committing to naming your priorities, spend five to 10 minutes writing or mapping a sketch of everything that's currently most important to you in your life. Don't edit yourself; it's okay if this list includes your most personal desires—good, bad, or otherwise. Be open and honest with yourself about where your heart is right now.

Now think about Jesus' top priority: loving others. How is Jesus' command connected to the most important things in your life? Pray about it. Challenge yourself to be open to what that really means for you. If being centered on Jesus is all about loving others, how will that affect your priorities? Make a list of your life's priorities here.

With Jesus' command in mind, prayerfully consider your top priority—what's the most important investment of your time and energy—for you to focus on for the next three months. Your priority can be anything: your family, job, friends, special project—whichever part of your life you want to be more centered on Jesus.

1ST QUARTER PRIORITY (JANUARY, FEBRUARY, MARCH)

Focusing on this priority is important to *you* because...

Focusing on this priority is important to *Jesus* because...

ACTION STEPS needed to stay focused...

If you've identified one or two other top priorities, write them here along with the reasons they're important and what you plan to do to keep them in focus.

To Do

Notes

Sunday	Monday	Tuesday
26	27	28
2	3	4
9	10	11
16	17 Martin Luther King Jr. Day	18
23	24	25
30	31	1

This month, keep your priorities focused on Jesus by...

	Wednesday	Thursday	Friday	Saturday
	29	30	31	1 New Year's Day
	5	6	7	8
	12	13	14	15
	19	20	21	22
	26	27	28	29
	2	3	4	5

Loving others: Loving others must always show up in your priorities. Who are you going to focus on loving this month? Write one to three names here, and schedule time to reach out to those people.

DEC 26 – JAN 1

26 Sunday	*27 Monday*	*28 Tuesday*	*29 Wednesday*
6:00	6:00	6:00	6:00
7:00	7:00	7:00	7:00
8:00	8:00	8:00	8:00
9:00	9:00	9:00	9:00
10:00	10:00	10:00	10:00
11:00	11:00	11:00	11:00
12:00	12:00	12:00	12:00
1:00	1:00	1:00	1:00
2:00	2:00	2:00	2:00
3:00	3:00	3:00	3:00
4:00	4:00	4:00	4:00
5:00	5:00	5:00	5:00
6:00	6:00	6:00	6:00
7:00	7:00	7:00	7:00
8:00	8:00	8:00	8:00
9:00	9:00	9:00	9:00
10:00	10:00	10:00	10:00

You bring out the best. Though the world is full of robust flavors, they leave an artificial aftertaste on the tongue. *But not you.* You're salt. Natural and authentic, you bring out the best flavors in those around you. You're my preserving agent, unlocking the true taste of the life you've found in me.

Love, Jesus

Matthew 5:13

30 Thursday	31 Friday	1 Saturday	What are your prayer priorities this week?
		READ *Genesis 1*	
6:00	6:00	6:00	
7:00	7:00	7:00	
8:00	8:00	8:00	
9:00	9:00	9:00	
10:00	10:00	10:00	
11:00	11:00	11:00	
12:00	12:00	12:00	
1:00	1:00	1:00	
2:00	2:00	2:00	
3:00	3:00	3:00	*To Do*
4:00	4:00	4:00	
5:00	5:00	5:00	
6:00	6:00	6:00	
7:00	7:00	7:00	
8:00	8:00	8:00	
9:00	9:00	9:00	
10:00	10:00	10:00	

Things you're thankful for this week:

2 Sunday	3 Monday	4 Tuesday	5 Wednesday
READ	READ	READ	READ
Genesis 2	*John 1*	*Genesis 3*	*Romans 3*
6:00	6:00	6:00	6:00
7:00	7:00	7:00	7:00
8:00	8:00	8:00	8:00
9:00	9:00	9:00	9:00
10:00	10:00	10:00	10:00
11:00	11:00	11:00	11:00
12:00	12:00	12:00	12:00
1:00	1:00	1:00	1:00
2:00	2:00	2:00	2:00
3:00	3:00	3:00	3:00
4:00	4:00	4:00	4:00
5:00	5:00	5:00	5:00
6:00	6:00	6:00	6:00
7:00	7:00	7:00	7:00
8:00	8:00	8:00	8:00
9:00	9:00	9:00	9:00
10:00	10:00	10:00	10:00

You destroy darkness. That fiend darkness, swallowing hope and extinguishing faith. It seems impenetrable, unstoppable. But not against you. You're a bright, blazing destroyer of darkness, crushing it with my light.

Love, Jesus

Matthew 5:14

6 Thursday

READ
Genesis 7

6:00

7:00

8:00

9:00

10:00

11:00

12:00

1:00

2:00

3:00

4:00

5:00

6:00

7:00

8:00

9:00

10:00

7 Friday

READ
Genesis 8

6:00

7:00

8:00

9:00

10:00

11:00

12:00

1:00

2:00

3:00

4:00

5:00

6:00

7:00

8:00

9:00

10:00

8 Saturday

READ
Genesis 12

6:00

7:00

8:00

9:00

10:00

11:00

12:00

1:00

2:00

3:00

4:00

5:00

6:00

7:00

8:00

9:00

10:00

What are your prayer priorities this week?

To Do

Things you're thankful for this week:

9 Sunday

READ
Malachi 4

6:00

7:00

8:00

9:00

10:00

11:00

12:00

1:00

2:00

3:00

4:00

5:00

6:00

7:00

8:00

9:00

10:00

10 Monday

READ
Mark 1

6:00

7:00

8:00

9:00

10:00

11:00

12:00

1:00

2:00

3:00

4:00

5:00

6:00

7:00

8:00

9:00

10:00

11 Tuesday

READ
Matthew 3

6:00

7:00

8:00

9:00

10:00

11:00

12:00

1:00

2:00

3:00

4:00

5:00

6:00

7:00

8:00

9:00

10:00

12 Wednesday

READ
Matthew 4

6:00

7:00

8:00

9:00

10:00

11:00

12:00

1:00

2:00

3:00

4:00

5:00

6:00

7:00

8:00

9:00

10:00

You keep things between us. When you honor me through your worship, generosity, and love, you aren't trying to impress others. I love this about you, because it doesn't matter what others think. Only my eyes matter, and only your heart matters. Let's keep things between us.

Love, Jesus

Matthew 6:4, 8, 18

13 Thursday	14 Friday	15 Saturday	What are your prayer priorities this week?
READ Mark 2	READ Mark 3	READ Mark 4	
6:00	6:00	6:00	....
7:00	7:00	7:00	....
8:00	8:00	8:00	....
9:00	9:00	9:00	....
10:00	10:00	10:00	....
11:00	11:00	11:00	....
12:00	12:00	12:00	....
1:00	1:00	1:00	....
2:00	2:00	2:00	....
3:00	3:00	3:00	To Do
4:00	4:00	4:00	....
5:00	5:00	5:00	....
6:00	6:00	6:00	....
7:00	7:00	7:00	....
8:00	8:00	8:00	....
9:00	9:00	9:00	....
10:00	10:00	10:00	....

Things you're thankful for this week:

JAN 16 – JAN 22

16 Sunday	*17 Monday*	*18 Tuesday*	*19 Wednesday*
READ	READ	READ	READ
Mark 5	*Mark 6*	*Mark 7*	*Mark 8*
6:00	6:00	6:00	6:00
7:00	7:00	7:00	7:00
8:00	8:00	8:00	8:00
9:00	9:00	9:00	9:00
10:00	10:00	10:00	10:00
11:00	11:00	11:00	11:00
12:00	12:00	12:00	12:00
1:00	1:00	1:00	1:00
2:00	2:00	2:00	2:00
3:00	3:00	3:00	3:00
4:00	4:00	4:00	4:00
5:00	5:00	5:00	5:00
6:00	6:00	6:00	6:00
7:00	7:00	7:00	7:00
8:00	8:00	8:00	8:00
9:00	9:00	9:00	9:00
10:00	10:00	10:00	10:00

You're outrageously carefree. Though it may not feel like it, you're outrageously carefree. Because I've provided for all your needs, you have no need for worry. *Ever.* This carefree spirit seems careless to the world, but don't let that diminish your levity. Embrace the freedom I offer, for it is an enviable gift.

Love, Jesus

Matthew 6:26

20 Thursday

READ
Mark 9

6:00

7:00

8:00

9:00

10:00

11:00

12:00

1:00

2:00

3:00

4:00

5:00

6:00

7:00

8:00

9:00

10:00

21 Friday

READ
Mark 10

6:00

7:00

8:00

9:00

10:00

11:00

12:00

1:00

2:00

3:00

4:00

5:00

6:00

7:00

8:00

9:00

10:00

22 Saturday

READ
Mark 11

6:00

7:00

8:00

9:00

10:00

11:00

12:00

1:00

2:00

3:00

4:00

5:00

6:00

7:00

8:00

9:00

10:00

What are your prayer priorities this week?

To Do

Things you're thankful for this week:

JAN 23 – JAN 29

23 Sunday
READ
Mark 12

6:00

7:00

8:00

9:00

10:00

11:00

12:00

1:00

2:00

3:00

4:00

5:00

6:00

7:00

8:00

9:00

10:00

24 Monday
READ
Mark 13

6:00

7:00

8:00

9:00

10:00

11:00

12:00

1:00

2:00

3:00

4:00

5:00

6:00

7:00

8:00

9:00

10:00

25 Tuesday
READ
Mark 14

6:00

7:00

8:00

9:00

10:00

11:00

12:00

1:00

2:00

3:00

4:00

5:00

6:00

7:00

8:00

9:00

10:00

26 Wednesday
READ
Mark 15

6:00

7:00

8:00

9:00

10:00

11:00

12:00

1:00

2:00

3:00

4:00

5:00

6:00

7:00

8:00

9:00

10:00

You're a child again. Through me, you have become *a child* of God. How long has it been since you've been given permission to be a kid—to play without restraint and create without obligation? Let me worry your worries and take on your responsibilities. Let me release you from adulthood to be a child again.

Love, Jesus

John 1:12

27 Thursday

READ
Mark 16

6:00

7:00

8:00

9:00

10:00

11:00

12:00

1:00

2:00

3:00

4:00

5:00

6:00

7:00

8:00

9:00

10:00

28 Friday

READ
Galatians 1

6:00

7:00

8:00

9:00

10:00

11:00

12:00

1:00

2:00

3:00

4:00

5:00

6:00

7:00

8:00

9:00

10:00

29 Saturday

READ
1 Timothy 1

6:00

7:00

8:00

9:00

10:00

11:00

12:00

1:00

2:00

3:00

4:00

5:00

6:00

7:00

8:00

9:00

10:00

What are your prayer priorities this week?

To Do

Things you're thankful for this week:

Review your gratitude notes from previous weeks, and write a prayer to Jesus thanking him for this month.

What experiences, insights, and moments helped keep Jesus a priority in your life in January? Record them here so you don't forget them.

Reviewing the previous month, how did focusing on the right priorities make a difference in your life?

Are there any ways you might adjust your priorities in the month ahead?

Review your appointments and tasks for the coming month. In what ways are they helping you focus on Jesus' priority of loving others? Is there anything you need to cancel, add, or change? Pray about it; then update your schedule as needed.

Now write a prayer thanking Jesus for new opportunities coming in February, including one way you're planning to stay focused on him.

To Do

- --------------------------------
- --------------------------------
- --------------------------------
- --------------------------------
- --------------------------------
- --------------------------------
- --------------------------------
- --------------------------------
- --------------------------------
- --------------------------------
- --------------------------------
- --------------------------------

Notes

Sunday	Monday	Tuesday
30	31	1
6	7	8
13	14 Valentine's Day	15
20	21 Presidents Day	22
27	28	1

This month, keep your priorities focused on Jesus by...

Wednesday	Thursday	Friday	Saturday
2	3	4	5
9	10	11	12
16	17	18	19
23	24	25	26
2	3	4	5

Loving others: Loving others must always show up in your priorities. Who are you going to show love to this month? Write one to three names here, and schedule time to reach out to those people.

30 Sunday	*31 Monday*	*1 Tuesday*	*2 Wednesday*
READ 2 Timothy 1	READ 2 Timothy 2	READ Isaiah 61	READ John 2
6:00	6:00	6:00	6:00
7:00	7:00	7:00	7:00
8:00	8:00	8:00	8:00
9:00	9:00	9:00	9:00
10:00	10:00	10:00	10:00
11:00	11:00	11:00	11:00
12:00	12:00	12:00	12:00
1:00	1:00	1:00	1:00
2:00	2:00	2:00	2:00
3:00	3:00	3:00	3:00
4:00	4:00	4:00	4:00
5:00	5:00	5:00	5:00
6:00	6:00	6:00	6:00
7:00	7:00	7:00	7:00
8:00	8:00	8:00	8:00
9:00	9:00	9:00	9:00
10:00	10:00	10:00	10:00

You have my Spirit. Your experience of being mortal—living in your body, dwelling on earth—is a shadow of what's true. My Spirit is the *full* truth. It's more spirit than flesh, more heaven than earth, more eternal than temporal. And it's growing stronger in you every day.

Love, Jesus

John 3:3-6

3 Thursday

READ

John 6

6:00

7:00

8:00

9:00

10:00

11:00

12:00

1:00

2:00

3:00

4:00

5:00

6:00

7:00

8:00

9:00

10:00

4 Friday

READ

Matthew 8

6:00

7:00

8:00

9:00

10:00

11:00

12:00

1:00

2:00

3:00

4:00

5:00

6:00

7:00

8:00

9:00

10:00

5 Saturday

READ

Matthew 9

6:00

7:00

8:00

9:00

10:00

11:00

12:00

1:00

2:00

3:00

4:00

5:00

6:00

7:00

8:00

9:00

10:00

What are your prayer priorities this week?

To Do

Things you're thankful for this week:

FEB 6 – FEB 12

6 Sunday	7 Monday	8 Tuesday	9 Wednesday
READ *Matthew 12*	READ *Matthew 14*	READ *Matthew 15*	READ *Matthew 17*
6:00	6:00	6:00	6:00
7:00	7:00	7:00	7:00
8:00	8:00	8:00	8:00
9:00	9:00	9:00	9:00
10:00	10:00	10:00	10:00
11:00	11:00	11:00	11:00
12:00	12:00	12:00	12:00
1:00	1:00	1:00	1:00
2:00	2:00	2:00	2:00
3:00	3:00	3:00	3:00
4:00	4:00	4:00	4:00
5:00	5:00	5:00	5:00
6:00	6:00	6:00	6:00
7:00	7:00	7:00	7:00
8:00	8:00	8:00	8:00
9:00	9:00	9:00	9:00
10:00	10:00	10:00	10:00

You're growing. When you're feeling dried up and brittle, remember who you're connected to, and stop trying to pull your own nourishment up from the ground. Put away your brittle self, and see the truth: As part of *my* root system, you are healthy, verdant, and growing.

Love, Jesus

John 15:1, 5

10 Thursday

READ
Matthew 20

6:00

7:00

8:00

9:00

10:00

11:00

12:00

1:00

2:00

3:00

4:00

5:00

6:00

7:00

8:00

9:00

10:00

11 Friday

READ
Matthew 21

6:00

7:00

8:00

9:00

10:00

11:00

12:00

1:00

2:00

3:00

4:00

5:00

6:00

7:00

8:00

9:00

10:00

12 Saturday

READ
Luke 3

6:00

7:00

8:00

9:00

10:00

11:00

12:00

1:00

2:00

3:00

4:00

5:00

6:00

7:00

8:00

9:00

10:00

What are your prayer priorities this week?

To Do

Things you're thankful for this week:

13 Sunday

READ
Luke 4

6:00

7:00

8:00

9:00

10:00

11:00

12:00

1:00

2:00

3:00

4:00

5:00

6:00

7:00

8:00

9:00

10:00

14 Monday

READ
Luke 5

6:00

7:00

8:00

9:00

10:00

11:00

12:00

1:00

2:00

3:00

4:00

5:00

6:00

7:00

8:00

9:00

10:00

15 Tuesday

READ
Luke 6

6:00

7:00

8:00

9:00

10:00

11:00

12:00

1:00

2:00

3:00

4:00

5:00

6:00

7:00

8:00

9:00

10:00

16 Wednesday

READ
Luke 7

6:00

7:00

8:00

9:00

10:00

11:00

12:00

1:00

2:00

3:00

4:00

5:00

6:00

7:00

8:00

9:00

10:00

You're my friend. As your friend, I'm *for* you. I don't tell your secrets. I don't leave you out. I'm not friends with you because I *have* to be but because I picked you. That's what friends do.

Love, Jesus

John 15:15

17 Thursday

READ
Luke 8

6:00

7:00

8:00

9:00

10:00

11:00

12:00

1:00

2:00

3:00

4:00

5:00

6:00

7:00

8:00

9:00

10:00

18 Friday

READ
Luke 9

6:00

7:00

8:00

9:00

10:00

11:00

12:00

1:00

2:00

3:00

4:00

5:00

6:00

7:00

8:00

9:00

10:00

19 Saturday

READ
Luke 10

6:00

7:00

8:00

9:00

10:00

11:00

12:00

1:00

2:00

3:00

4:00

5:00

6:00

7:00

8:00

9:00

10:00

What are your prayer priorities this week?

To Do

Things you're thankful for this week:

20 Sunday

READ
Exodus 4

6:00

7:00

8:00

9:00

10:00

11:00

12:00

1:00

2:00

3:00

4:00

5:00

6:00

7:00

8:00

9:00

10:00

21 Monday

READ
Exodus 16

6:00

7:00

8:00

9:00

10:00

11:00

12:00

1:00

2:00

3:00

4:00

5:00

6:00

7:00

8:00

9:00

10:00

22 Tuesday

READ
Exodus 17

6:00

7:00

8:00

9:00

10:00

11:00

12:00

1:00

2:00

3:00

4:00

5:00

6:00

7:00

8:00

9:00

10:00

23 Wednesday

READ
1 Kings 17

6:00

7:00

8:00

9:00

10:00

11:00

12:00

1:00

2:00

3:00

4:00

5:00

6:00

7:00

8:00

9:00

10:00

You're free. That sneering, critical voice in your head is a false warden holding you captive, counting on your compliance. But haven't you heard? I've set you free! You can walk right out of that cell you've put yourself in. Just open the door.

Love, Jesus

Romans 8:1

24 Thursday

READND
1 Kings 18

6:00

7:00

8:00

9:00

10:00

11:00

12:00

1:00

2:00

3:00

4:00

5:00

6:00

7:00

8:00

9:00

10:00

25 Friday

READ
2 Kings 2

6:00

7:00

8:00

9:00

10:00

11:00

12:00

1:00

2:00

3:00

4:00

5:00

6:00

7:00

8:00

9:00

10:00

26 Saturday

READ
Daniel 3

6:00

7:00

8:00

9:00

10:00

11:00

12:00

1:00

2:00

3:00

4:00

5:00

6:00

7:00

8:00

9:00

10:00

What are your prayer priorities this week?

To Do

Things you're thankful for this week:

Review your gratitude notes from previous weeks, and write a prayer to Jesus thanking him for this month.

What experiences, insights, and moments helped keep Jesus a priority in your life in February? Record them here so you don't forget them.

Reviewing the previous month, how did focusing on the right priorities make a difference in your life?

Are there any ways you might adjust your priorities in the month ahead?

Review your appointments and tasks for the coming month. In what ways are they helping you focus on Jesus' priority of loving others? Is there anything you need to cancel, add, or change? Pray about it; then update your schedule as needed.

Now write a prayer thanking Jesus for new opportunities coming in March, and include one way you're planning to stay focused on him.

To Do

_____
_____
_____
_____
_____
_____
_____
_____
_____
_____
_____
_____

Notes

MARCH 2022

Sunday	Monday	Tuesday
27	28	1
6	7	8
13	14	15
20	21	22
27	28	29

This month, keep your priorities focused on Jesus by...

_____
_____
_____
_____
_____
_____
_____
_____
_____
_____
_____

Wednesday	Thursday	Friday	Saturday
2	3	4	5
9	10	11	12
16	17	18	19
23	24	25	26
30	31	1	2

Loving others: Loving others must always show up in your priorities. Who are you going to show love to this month? Write one to three names here, and schedule time to reach out to those people.

27 Sunday
READ
Daniel 6

6:00

7:00

8:00

9:00

10:00

11:00

12:00

1:00

2:00

3:00

4:00

5:00

6:00

7:00

8:00

9:00

10:00

28 Monday
READ
Psalm 92

6:00

7:00

8:00

9:00

10:00

11:00

12:00

1:00

2:00

3:00

4:00

5:00

6:00

7:00

8:00

9:00

10:00

1 Tuesday
READ
Genesis 22

6:00

7:00

8:00

9:00

10:00

11:00

12:00

1:00

2:00

3:00

4:00

5:00

6:00

7:00

8:00

9:00

10:00

2 Wednesday
READ
Isaiah 50

6:00

7:00

8:00

9:00

10:00

11:00

12:00

1:00

2:00

3:00

4:00

5:00

6:00

7:00

8:00

9:00

10:00

You're in a spacious place. Rules are bullies. They push you around, cramming you into a mold that looks good on the outside but squeezes your heart. My way is different. It's a mold that fits you perfectly—open, spacious, *right*.

Love, Jesus

Romans 8:2

3 Thursday	4 Friday	5 Saturday	What are your prayer priorities this week?
READ *Isaiah 53*	READ *Isaiah 59*	READ *Matthew 26*	

3 Thursday	4 Friday	5 Saturday
6:00	6:00	6:00
7:00	7:00	7:00
8:00	8:00	8:00
9:00	9:00	9:00
10:00	10:00	10:00
11:00	11:00	11:00
12:00	12:00	12:00
1:00	1:00	1:00
2:00	2:00	2:00
3:00	3:00	3:00
4:00	4:00	4:00
5:00	5:00	5:00
6:00	6:00	6:00
7:00	7:00	7:00
8:00	8:00	8:00
9:00	9:00	9:00
10:00	10:00	10:00

To Do

Things you're thankful for this week:

6 Sunday

READ
Matthew 27

6:00

7:00

8:00

9:00

10:00

11:00

12:00

1:00

2:00

3:00

4:00

5:00

6:00

7:00

8:00

9:00

10:00

7 Monday

READ
Psalm 22

6:00

7:00

8:00

9:00

10:00

11:00

12:00

1:00

2:00

3:00

4:00

5:00

6:00

7:00

8:00

9:00

10:00

8 Tuesday

READ
Zechariah 12

6:00

7:00

8:00

9:00

10:00

11:00

12:00

1:00

2:00

3:00

4:00

5:00

6:00

7:00

8:00

9:00

10:00

9 Wednesday

READ
John 12

6:00

7:00

8:00

9:00

10:00

11:00

12:00

1:00

2:00

3:00

4:00

5:00

6:00

7:00

8:00

9:00

10:00

You're my heir. You're heir to the King and all the riches of his kingdom. Heirs do not inherit by merit but by blood. *My* blood. You're also heir to something else you'd rather forget: my suffering. It doesn't make sense for you to inherit such a thing, but it offers a mysterious reward.

Love, Jesus

Romans 8:17

10 Thursday

READ
John 13

6:00

7:00

8:00

9:00

10:00

11:00

12:00

1:00

2:00

3:00

4:00

5:00

6:00

7:00

8:00

9:00

10:00

11 Friday

READ
John 18

6:00

7:00

8:00

9:00

10:00

11:00

12:00

1:00

2:00

3:00

4:00

5:00

6:00

7:00

8:00

9:00

10:00

12 Saturday

READ
John 19

6:00

7:00

8:00

9:00

10:00

11:00

12:00

1:00

2:00

3:00

4:00

5:00

6:00

7:00

8:00

9:00

10:00

What are your prayer priorities this week?

To Do

Things you're thankful for this week:

13 Sunday	*14 Monday*	*15 Tuesday*	*16 Wednesday*
READ	READ	READ	READ
Galatians 2	*Matthew 10*	*1 Corinthians 1*	*1 Peter 2*
6:00	6:00	6:00	6:00
7:00	7:00	7:00	7:00
8:00	8:00	8:00	8:00
9:00	9:00	9:00	9:00
10:00	10:00	10:00	10:00
11:00	11:00	11:00	11:00
12:00	12:00	12:00	12:00
1:00	1:00	1:00	1:00
2:00	2:00	2:00	2:00
3:00	3:00	3:00	3:00
4:00	4:00	4:00	4:00
5:00	5:00	5:00	5:00
6:00	6:00	6:00	6:00
7:00	7:00	7:00	7:00
8:00	8:00	8:00	8:00
9:00	9:00	9:00	9:00
10:00	10:00	10:00	10:00

You're a victor. Sometimes it feels like you're losing the battle. Losing to cancer, to failure. Losing to love gone sour. But hold on. I have a secret: The game is rigged. Losing is winning when I set the rules, and I've already won this game.

Love, Jesus

Romans 8:37

17 Thursday

READ
Matthew 16

6:00

7:00

8:00

9:00

10:00

11:00

12:00

1:00

2:00

3:00

4:00

5:00

6:00

7:00

8:00

9:00

10:00

18 Friday

READ
2 Corinthians 5

6:00

7:00

8:00

9:00

10:00

11:00

12:00

1:00

2:00

3:00

4:00

5:00

6:00

7:00

8:00

9:00

10:00

19 Saturday

READ
Galatians 3

6:00

7:00

8:00

9:00

10:00

11:00

12:00

1:00

2:00

3:00

4:00

5:00

6:00

7:00

8:00

9:00

10:00

What are your prayer priorities this week?

To Do

Things you're thankful for this week:

20 Sunday

READ
1 Thessalonians 5

6:00

7:00

8:00

9:00

10:00

11:00

12:00

1:00

2:00

3:00

4:00

5:00

6:00

7:00

8:00

9:00

10:00

21 Monday

READ
Luke 20

6:00

7:00

8:00

9:00

10:00

11:00

12:00

1:00

2:00

3:00

4:00

5:00

6:00

7:00

8:00

9:00

10:00

22 Tuesday

READ
Luke 21

6:00

7:00

8:00

9:00

10:00

11:00

12:00

1:00

2:00

3:00

4:00

5:00

6:00

7:00

8:00

9:00

10:00

23 Wednesday

READ
Luke 22

6:00

7:00

8:00

9:00

10:00

11:00

12:00

1:00

2:00

3:00

4:00

5:00

6:00

7:00

8:00

9:00

10:00

You're welcome as you are. You're welcome at my table just as you are. You don't have to clean up, dress up, or shape up. I ask that you receive others the same way, just as they are. Extend your heart to them and begin to see them the way I do.

Love, Jesus

Romans 15:7

24 Thursday

READ
Luke 23

6:00

7:00

8:00

9:00

10:00

11:00

12:00

1:00

2:00

3:00

4:00

5:00

6:00

7:00

8:00

9:00

10:00

25 Friday

READ
Deuteronomy 21

6:00

7:00

8:00

9:00

10:00

11:00

12:00

1:00

2:00

3:00

4:00

5:00

6:00

7:00

8:00

9:00

10:00

26 Saturday

READ
Leviticus 16

6:00

7:00

8:00

9:00

10:00

11:00

12:00

1:00

2:00

3:00

4:00

5:00

6:00

7:00

8:00

9:00

10:00

What are your prayer priorities this week?

To Do

Things you're thankful for this week:

27 Sunday

READ
Leviticus 23

6:00

7:00

8:00

9:00

10:00

11:00

12:00

1:00

2:00

3:00

4:00

5:00

6:00

7:00

8:00

9:00

10:00

28 Monday

READ
Psalm 32

6:00

7:00

8:00

9:00

10:00

11:00

12:00

1:00

2:00

3:00

4:00

5:00

6:00

7:00

8:00

9:00

10:00

29 Tuesday

READ
Psalm 42

6:00

7:00

8:00

9:00

10:00

11:00

12:00

1:00

2:00

3:00

4:00

5:00

6:00

7:00

8:00

9:00

10:00

30 Wednesday

READ
Psalm 65

6:00

7:00

8:00

9:00

10:00

11:00

12:00

1:00

2:00

3:00

4:00

5:00

6:00

7:00

8:00

9:00

10:00

You're on the right track. I'm cheering for you. Those things in your heart—I care about them, too. That vision you see—pursue it. Those obstacles you encounter—persevere. Nothing can stand in your way when I'm for you.

Love, Jesus

Romans 8:31-32

31 Thursday	1 Friday	2 Saturday
READ	READ	READ
Hosea 14	*Matthew 28*	*Luke 24*
6:00	6:00	6:00
7:00	7:00	7:00
8:00	8:00	8:00
9:00	9:00	9:00
10:00	10:00	10:00
11:00	11:00	11:00
12:00	12:00	12:00
1:00	1:00	1:00
2:00	2:00	2:00
3:00	3:00	3:00
4:00	4:00	4:00
5:00	5:00	5:00
6:00	6:00	6:00
7:00	7:00	7:00
8:00	8:00	8:00
9:00	9:00	9:00
10:00	10:00	10:00

What are your prayer priorities this week?

To Do

Things you're thankful for this week:

Review your gratitude notes from previous weeks, and write a prayer to Jesus thanking him for this month.

What experiences, insights, and moments helped keep Jesus a priority in your life in March? Record them here so you don't forget them.

Reviewing the previous month, how did focusing on the right priorities make a difference in your life?

Are there any ways you might adjust your priorities in the month ahead?

Review your appointments and tasks for the coming month. In what ways are they helping you focus on Jesus' priority of loving others? Is there anything you need to cancel, add, or change? Pray about it; then update your schedule as needed.

Now write a prayer thanking Jesus for new opportunities coming in April, and include one way you're planning to stay focused on him.

Setting Jesus-Centered Priorities, Second Quarter

Look to Jesus' example to guide your life's priorities.

Before committing to naming your priorities, spend five to 10 minutes writing or mapping a sketch of everything that's currently most important to you in your life. Don't edit yourself; it's okay if this list includes your most personal desires—good, bad, or otherwise. Be open and honest with yourself about where your heart is right now.

Now think about Jesus' top priority: loving others. How is Jesus' command connected to the most important things in your life? Pray about it. Challenge yourself to be open to what that really means for you. If being centered on Jesus is all about loving others, how will that affect your priorities? Make a list of your life's priorities here.

With Jesus' command in mind, prayerfully consider your top priority—what's the most important investment of your time and energy—for you to focus on for the next three months. Your priority can be anything: your family, job, friends, special project—whichever part of your life you want to be more centered on Jesus.

2ND QUARTER PRIORITY (APRIL, MAY, JUNE)

Focusing on this priority is important to *you* because…

Focusing on this priority is important to *Jesus* because…

ACTION STEPS needed to stay focused…

If you've identified one or two other top priorities, write them here along with the reasons they're important and what you plan to do to keep them in focus.

To Do

Sunday	Monday	Tuesday
27	28	29
3	4	5
10	11	12
Palm Sunday		
17	18	19
Easter Sunday		
24	25	26

Notes

This month, keep your priorities focused on Jesus by...

Wednesday	Thursday	Friday	Saturday
30	31	1	2
6	7	8	9
13	14	15 Good Friday	16
20	21	22	23
27	28	29	30

Loving others: Loving others must always show up in your priorities.
Who are you going to show love to this month? Write one to three names
here, and schedule time to reach out to those people.

APR 3 – APR 9

3 Sunday

READ
John 11

6:00

7:00

8:00

9:00

10:00

11:00

12:00

1:00

2:00

3:00

4:00

5:00

6:00

7:00

8:00

9:00

10:00

4 Monday

READ
John 20

6:00

7:00

8:00

9:00

10:00

11:00

12:00

1:00

2:00

3:00

4:00

5:00

6:00

7:00

8:00

9:00

10:00

5 Tuesday

READ
John 21

6:00

7:00

8:00

9:00

10:00

11:00

12:00

1:00

2:00

3:00

4:00

5:00

6:00

7:00

8:00

9:00

10:00

6 Wednesday

READ
1 Corinthians 6

6:00

7:00

8:00

9:00

10:00

11:00

12:00

1:00

2:00

3:00

4:00

5:00

6:00

7:00

8:00

9:00

10:00

You're wise when others are foolish. You have wisdom that's not from this world. You give when you should keep, serve when you should lead, surrender when you should fight. I cherish this wisdom because it comes from me. It is the true path that exposes foolishness masquerading as good sense.

Love, Jesus

1 Corinthians 1:30

7 Thursday

READ
1 Corinthians 15

6:00

7:00

8:00

9:00

10:00

11:00

12:00

1:00

2:00

3:00

4:00

5:00

6:00

7:00

8:00

9:00

10:00

8 Friday

READ
Daniel 12

6:00

7:00

8:00

9:00

10:00

11:00

12:00

1:00

2:00

3:00

4:00

5:00

6:00

7:00

8:00

9:00

10:00

9 Saturday

READ
Matthew 22

6:00

7:00

8:00

9:00

10:00

11:00

12:00

1:00

2:00

3:00

4:00

5:00

6:00

7:00

8:00

9:00

10:00

What are your prayer priorities this week?

To Do

Things you're thankful for this week:

10 Sunday

READ
Matthew 24

6:00

7:00

8:00

9:00

10:00

11:00

12:00

1:00

2:00

3:00

4:00

5:00

6:00

7:00

8:00

9:00

10:00

11 Monday

READ
Job 19

6:00

7:00

8:00

9:00

10:00

11:00

12:00

1:00

2:00

3:00

4:00

5:00

6:00

7:00

8:00

9:00

10:00

12 Tuesday

READ
Ezekiel 11

6:00

7:00

8:00

9:00

10:00

11:00

12:00

1:00

2:00

3:00

4:00

5:00

6:00

7:00

8:00

9:00

10:00

13 Wednesday

READ
Isaiah 25

6:00

7:00

8:00

9:00

10:00

11:00

12:00

1:00

2:00

3:00

4:00

5:00

6:00

7:00

8:00

9:00

10:00

You make spaces sacred. My Spirit within you cannot be contained. You bring my presence with you wherever you go, turning mundane places into sacred spaces. I don't need your invitation or permission to come—you've already brought me here.

Love, Jesus

1 Corinthians 6:19

14 Thursday

READ
2 Thessalonians 2

6:00

7:00

8:00

9:00

10:00

11:00

12:00

1:00

2:00

3:00

4:00

5:00

6:00

7:00

8:00

9:00

10:00

15 Friday

READ
Psalm 118

6:00

7:00

8:00

9:00

10:00

11:00

12:00

1:00

2:00

3:00

4:00

5:00

6:00

7:00

8:00

9:00

10:00

16 Saturday

READ
Isaiah 26

6:00

7:00

8:00

9:00

10:00

11:00

12:00

1:00

2:00

3:00

4:00

5:00

6:00

7:00

8:00

9:00

10:00

What are your prayer priorities this week?

To Do

Things you're thankful for this week:

17 Sunday
READ
Isaiah 65

6:00
7:00
8:00
9:00
10:00
11:00
12:00
1:00
2:00
3:00
4:00
5:00
6:00
7:00
8:00
9:00
10:00

18 Monday
READ
2 Kings 4

6:00
7:00
8:00
9:00
10:00
11:00
12:00
1:00
2:00
3:00
4:00
5:00
6:00
7:00
8:00
9:00
10:00

19 Tuesday
READ
2 Kings 13

6:00
7:00
8:00
9:00
10:00
11:00
12:00
1:00
2:00
3:00
4:00
5:00
6:00
7:00
8:00
9:00
10:00

20 Wednesday
READ
2 Peter 3

6:00
7:00
8:00
9:00
10:00
11:00
12:00
1:00
2:00
3:00
4:00
5:00
6:00
7:00
8:00
9:00
10:00

You're becoming new. It gets old being the *old* you, doesn't it? Stuck in patterns, letting others down, rinse and repeat. Here's what I offer instead: a new you with new patterns. *My patterns.* I promise they'll never get old.

Love, Jesus

2 Corinthians 5:17

21 Thursday

READ
Revelation 1

6:00

7:00

8:00

9:00

10:00

11:00

12:00

1:00

2:00

3:00

4:00

5:00

6:00

7:00

8:00

9:00

10:00

22 Friday

READ
Revelation 2

6:00

7:00

8:00

9:00

10:00

11:00

12:00

1:00

2:00

3:00

4:00

5:00

6:00

7:00

8:00

9:00

10:00

23 Saturday

READ
Revelation 3

6:00

7:00

8:00

9:00

10:00

11:00

12:00

1:00

2:00

3:00

4:00

5:00

6:00

7:00

8:00

9:00

10:00

What are your prayer priorities this week?

To Do

Things you're thankful for this week:

APR 24 – APR 30

24 Sunday

READ
Revelation 4

6:00

7:00

8:00

9:00

10:00

11:00

12:00

1:00

2:00

3:00

4:00

5:00

6:00

7:00

8:00

9:00

10:00

25 Monday

READ
Revelation 5

6:00

7:00

8:00

9:00

10:00

11:00

12:00

1:00

2:00

3:00

4:00

5:00

6:00

7:00

8:00

9:00

10:00

26 Tuesday

READ
Revelation 6

6:00

7:00

8:00

9:00

10:00

11:00

12:00

1:00

2:00

3:00

4:00

5:00

6:00

7:00

8:00

9:00

10:00

27 Wednesday

READ
Revelation 7

6:00

7:00

8:00

9:00

10:00

11:00

12:00

1:00

2:00

3:00

4:00

5:00

6:00

7:00

8:00

9:00

10:00

You're fresh life. Bad words, attitudes, and ideas fill the air like a pungent smell. But then you enter, and you're like the very essence of spring. Like a natural purifier, your words bring life, freshening those around you like newly cut grass and crisp spring air.

Love, Jesus

Romans 8:31-32

28 Thursday

READ
Revelation 20

6:00

7:00

8:00

9:00

10:00

11:00

12:00

1:00

2:00

3:00

4:00

5:00

6:00

7:00

8:00

9:00

10:00

29 Friday

READ
Revelation 21

6:00

7:00

8:00

9:00

10:00

11:00

12:00

1:00

2:00

3:00

4:00

5:00

6:00

7:00

8:00

9:00

10:00

30 Saturday

READ
Revelation 22

6:00

7:00

8:00

9:00

10:00

11:00

12:00

1:00

2:00

3:00

4:00

5:00

6:00

7:00

8:00

9:00

10:00

What are your prayer priorities this week?

To Do

Things you're thankful for this week:

Review your gratitude notes from previous weeks, and write a prayer to Jesus thanking him for this month.

What experiences, insights, and moments helped keep Jesus a priority in your life in April? Record them here so you don't forget them.

Reviewing the previous month, how did focusing on the right priorities make a difference in your life?

Are there any ways you might adjust your priorities in the month ahead?

Review your appointments and tasks for the coming month. In what ways are they helping you focus on Jesus' priority of loving others? Is there anything you need to cancel, add, or change? Pray about it; then update your schedule as needed.

Now write a prayer thanking Jesus for new opportunities coming in May, and include one way you're planning to stay focused on him.

To Do

Sunday	Monday	Tuesday
1	2	3
8 Mother's Day	9	10
15	16	17
22	23	24
29	30 Memorial Day	31

Notes

This month, keep your priorities focused on Jesus by...

Wednesday	Thursday	Friday	Saturday
4	5	6	7
11	12	13	14
18	19	20	21
25	26	27	28
1	2	3	4

Loving others: Loving others must always show up in your priorities. Who are you going to focus on loving this month? Write one to three names here, and schedule time to reach out to those people.

MAY 1 – MAY 7

1 Sunday

READ
Acts 1

6:00

7:00

8:00

9:00

10:00

11:00

12:00

1:00

2:00

3:00

4:00

5:00

6:00

7:00

8:00

9:00

10:00

2 Monday

READ
Acts 2

6:00

7:00

8:00

9:00

10:00

11:00

12:00

1:00

2:00

3:00

4:00

5:00

6:00

7:00

8:00

9:00

10:00

3 Tuesday

READ
Acts 3

6:00

7:00

8:00

9:00

10:00

11:00

12:00

1:00

2:00

3:00

4:00

5:00

6:00

7:00

8:00

9:00

10:00

4 Wednesday

READ
Acts 4

6:00

7:00

8:00

9:00

10:00

11:00

12:00

1:00

2:00

3:00

4:00

5:00

6:00

7:00

8:00

9:00

10:00

You're my crack of light. Some people are completely closed to me. But not you. You're open. You hope, you wait, you believe against reason. You're my crack of light in a closed world.

Love, Jesus

2 Corinthians 3:14

5 Thursday

READ
Acts 5

6:00

7:00

8:00

9:00

10:00

11:00

12:00

1:00

2:00

3:00

4:00

5:00

6:00

7:00

8:00

9:00

10:00

6 Friday

READ
Acts 6

6:00

7:00

8:00

9:00

10:00

11:00

12:00

1:00

2:00

3:00

4:00

5:00

6:00

7:00

8:00

9:00

10:00

7 Saturday

READ
Acts 7

6:00

7:00

8:00

9:00

10:00

11:00

12:00

1:00

2:00

3:00

4:00

5:00

6:00

7:00

8:00

9:00

10:00

What are your prayer priorities this week?

To Do

Things you're thankful for this week:

8 Sunday	9 Monday	10 Tuesday	11 Wednesday
READ	READ	READ	READ
Acts 8	*Acts 9*	*Acts 10*	*Acts 11*
6:00	6:00	6:00	6:00
7:00	7:00	7:00	7:00
8:00	8:00	8:00	8:00
9:00	9:00	9:00	9:00
10:00	10:00	10:00	10:00
11:00	11:00	11:00	11:00
12:00	12:00	12:00	12:00
1:00	1:00	1:00	1:00
2:00	2:00	2:00	2:00
3:00	3:00	3:00	3:00
4:00	4:00	4:00	4:00
5:00	5:00	5:00	5:00
6:00	6:00	6:00	6:00
7:00	7:00	7:00	7:00
8:00	8:00	8:00	8:00
9:00	9:00	9:00	9:00
10:00	10:00	10:00	10:00

You're weak (and that's okay). All this work you're putting into getting it all together isn't working. No matter what you do, you're still fragile and flawed and sinful and selfish. So quit trying so hard, and be weak instead. Let me be the strong one. I'm better at it.

Love, Jesus

2 Corinthians 12:7-9

12 Thursday

READ
Acts 12

6:00

7:00

8:00

9:00

10:00

11:00

12:00

1:00

2:00

3:00

4:00

5:00

6:00

7:00

8:00

9:00

10:00

13 Friday

READ
Acts 13

6:00

7:00

8:00

9:00

10:00

11:00

12:00

1:00

2:00

3:00

4:00

5:00

6:00

7:00

8:00

9:00

10:00

14 Saturday

READ
Acts 14

6:00

7:00

8:00

9:00

10:00

11:00

12:00

1:00

2:00

3:00

4:00

5:00

6:00

7:00

8:00

9:00

10:00

What are your prayer priorities this week?

To Do

Things you're thankful for this week:

15 Sunday
READ
Acts 15

6:00
7:00
8:00
9:00
10:00
11:00
12:00
1:00
2:00
3:00
4:00
5:00
6:00
7:00
8:00
9:00
10:00

16 Monday
READ
Acts 16

6:00
7:00
8:00
9:00
10:00
11:00
12:00
1:00
2:00
3:00
4:00
5:00
6:00
7:00
8:00
9:00
10:00

17 Tuesday
READ
Acts 17

6:00
7:00
8:00
9:00
10:00
11:00
12:00
1:00
2:00
3:00
4:00
5:00
6:00
7:00
8:00
9:00
10:00

18 Wednesday
READ
Acts 18

6:00
7:00
8:00
9:00
10:00
11:00
12:00
1:00
2:00
3:00
4:00
5:00
6:00
7:00
8:00
9:00
10:00

You're trusting. It's audacious to trust in someone you can't see or touch, but you do it anyway. Every day you entrust your life—your eternity—to me. I'll prove to you again and again that I'm trustworthy, and I welcome you into the great and marvelous risk of taking me at my word.

Love, Jesus

Galatians 2:20

19 Thursday

READ
Acts 19

6:00

7:00

8:00

9:00

10:00

11:00

12:00

1:00

2:00

3:00

4:00

5:00

6:00

7:00

8:00

9:00

10:00

20 Friday

READ
Acts 20

6:00

7:00

8:00

9:00

10:00

11:00

12:00

1:00

2:00

3:00

4:00

5:00

6:00

7:00

8:00

9:00

10:00

21 Saturday

READ
Acts 21

6:00

7:00

8:00

9:00

10:00

11:00

12:00

1:00

2:00

3:00

4:00

5:00

6:00

7:00

8:00

9:00

10:00

What are your prayer priorities this week?

....

....

....

....

....

....

....

....

To Do

....

....

....

....

....

....

....

....

Things you're thankful for this week:

22 *Sunday*	23 *Monday*	24 *Tuesday*	25 *Wednesday*
READ *Acts 22*	READ *Acts 23*	READ *Acts 24*	READ *Acts 25*
6:00	6:00	6:00	6:00
7:00	7:00	7:00	7:00
8:00	8:00	8:00	8:00
9:00	9:00	9:00	9:00
10:00	10:00	10:00	10:00
11:00	11:00	11:00	11:00
12:00	12:00	12:00	12:00
1:00	1:00	1:00	1:00
2:00	2:00	2:00	2:00
3:00	3:00	3:00	3:00
4:00	4:00	4:00	4:00
5:00	5:00	5:00	5:00
6:00	6:00	6:00	6:00
7:00	7:00	7:00	7:00
8:00	8:00	8:00	8:00
9:00	9:00	9:00	9:00
10:00	10:00	10:00	10:00

You're with me. Don't waste your time on comparisons. Whether you're better or worse or different or the same, it doesn't matter. There are no outsiders—there's just me and those who are with me. We are one spirit and one group, including you.

Love, Jesus

Galatians 3:28

26 Thursday

READ
Acts 26

6:00

7:00

8:00

9:00

10:00

11:00

12:00

1:00

2:00

3:00

4:00

5:00

6:00

7:00

8:00

9:00

10:00

27 Friday

READ
Acts 27

6:00

7:00

8:00

9:00

10:00

11:00

12:00

1:00

2:00

3:00

4:00

5:00

6:00

7:00

8:00

9:00

10:00

28 Saturday

READ
Acts 28

6:00

7:00

8:00

9:00

10:00

11:00

12:00

1:00

2:00

3:00

4:00

5:00

6:00

7:00

8:00

9:00

10:00

What are your prayer priorities this week?

To Do

Things you're thankful for this week:

Review your gratitude notes from previous weeks, and write a prayer to Jesus thanking him for this month.

What experiences, insights, and moments helped keep Jesus a priority in your life in May? Record them here so you don't forget them.

Reviewing the previous month, how did focusing on the right priorities make a difference in your life?

Are there any ways you might adjust your priorities in the month ahead?

Review your appointments and tasks for the coming month. In what ways are they helping you focus on Jesus' priority of loving others? Is there anything you need to cancel, add, or change? Pray about it; then update your schedule as needed.

Now write a prayer thanking Jesus for new opportunities coming in June, and include one way you're planning to stay focused on him.

JUNE 2022

Sunday	Monday	Tuesday
29	30	31
5	6	7
12	13	14
19	20	21
Father's Day 26	27	28

To Do

- -
- -
- -
- -
- -
- -
- -
- -
- -
- -
- -
- -
- -
- -

Notes

This month, keep your priorities focused on Jesus by...

Wednesday	Thursday	Friday	Saturday
1	2	3	4
8	9	10	11
15	16	17	18
22	23	24	25
29	30	1	2

Loving others: Loving others must always show up in your priorities. Who are you going to show love to this month? Write one to three names here, and schedule time to reach out to those people.

29 Sunday	*30 Monday*	*31 Tuesday*	*1 Wednesday*
READ	READ	READ	READ
Jonah 1	*Jonah 2*	*Jonah 3*	*John 3*
6:00	6:00	6:00	6:00
7:00	7:00	7:00	7:00
8:00	8:00	8:00	8:00
9:00	9:00	9:00	9:00
10:00	10:00	10:00	10:00
11:00	11:00	11:00	11:00
12:00	12:00	12:00	12:00
1:00	1:00	1:00	1:00
2:00	2:00	2:00	2:00
3:00	3:00	3:00	3:00
4:00	4:00	4:00	4:00
5:00	5:00	5:00	5:00
6:00	6:00	6:00	6:00
7:00	7:00	7:00	7:00
8:00	8:00	8:00	8:00
9:00	9:00	9:00	9:00
10:00	10:00	10:00	10:00

You're overflowing. Left alone, you'll always come up short. Short on time, on discipline, on patience. But when you come up short, that's when I begin. So quit believing that you're empty. I'm overflowing, and there's plenty to go around.

Love, Jesus

Ephesians 1:3

2 Thursday	3 Friday	4 Saturday
READ	READ	READ
John 4	*John 5*	*Galatians 5*
6:00	6:00	6:00
7:00	7:00	7:00
8:00	8:00	8:00
9:00	9:00	9:00
10:00	10:00	10:00
11:00	11:00	11:00
12:00	12:00	12:00
1:00	1:00	1:00
2:00	2:00	2:00
3:00	3:00	3:00
4:00	4:00	4:00
5:00	5:00	5:00
6:00	6:00	6:00
7:00	7:00	7:00
8:00	8:00	8:00
9:00	9:00	9:00
10:00	10:00	10:00

What are your prayer priorities this week?

To Do

Things you're thankful for this week:

JUNE 5 – JUNE 11

5 Sunday	6 Monday	7 Tuesday	8 Wednesday
READ	READ	READ	READ
Galatians 6	*1 Peter 1*	*1 Peter 4*	*Romans 5*
6:00	6:00	6:00	6:00
7:00	7:00	7:00	7:00
8:00	8:00	8:00	8:00
9:00	9:00	9:00	9:00
10:00	10:00	10:00	10:00
11:00	11:00	11:00	11:00
12:00	12:00	12:00	12:00
1:00	1:00	1:00	1:00
2:00	2:00	2:00	2:00
3:00	3:00	3:00	3:00
4:00	4:00	4:00	4:00
5:00	5:00	5:00	5:00
6:00	6:00	6:00	6:00
7:00	7:00	7:00	7:00
8:00	8:00	8:00	8:00
9:00	9:00	9:00	9:00
10:00	10:00	10:00	10:00

You represent me. A name marks you, showing who you are and whose you are. You're [insert your first name], the Christ-follower. As you go, make disciples, teach, and obey in my name, remember this. I'm with you.

Love, Jesus

Matthew 28:18-20

9 Thursday

READ
Romans 6

6:00

7:00

8:00

9:00

10:00

11:00

12:00

1:00

2:00

3:00

4:00

5:00

6:00

7:00

8:00

9:00

10:00

10 Friday

READ
Romans 7

6:00

7:00

8:00

9:00

10:00

11:00

12:00

1:00

2:00

3:00

4:00

5:00

6:00

7:00

8:00

9:00

10:00

11 Saturday

READ
Romans 8

6:00

7:00

8:00

9:00

10:00

11:00

12:00

1:00

2:00

3:00

4:00

5:00

6:00

7:00

8:00

9:00

10:00

What are your prayer priorities this week?

To Do

Things you're thankful for this week:

JUNE 12 – JUNE 18

12 Sunday

READ
Ezekiel 37

6:00

7:00

8:00

9:00

10:00

11:00

12:00

1:00

2:00

3:00

4:00

5:00

6:00

7:00

8:00

9:00

10:00

13 Monday

READ
2 Timothy 3

6:00

7:00

8:00

9:00

10:00

11:00

12:00

1:00

2:00

3:00

4:00

5:00

6:00

7:00

8:00

9:00

10:00

14 Tuesday

READ
Matthew 5

6:00

7:00

8:00

9:00

10:00

11:00

12:00

1:00

2:00

3:00

4:00

5:00

6:00

7:00

8:00

9:00

10:00

15 Wednesday

READ
Matthew 6

6:00

7:00

8:00

9:00

10:00

11:00

12:00

1:00

2:00

3:00

4:00

5:00

6:00

7:00

8:00

9:00

10:00

You're forgiven. There will be times you let me down. Times you let down the people you love. Times you hurt, wound, afflict, offend. But for each of these times, I heal, restore, redeem, and forgive. My grace covers your sin, and it is more than enough.

Love, Jesus

Ephesians 1:7

16 Thursday

READ
Matthew 7

6:00

7:00

8:00

9:00

10:00

11:00

12:00

1:00

2:00

3:00

4:00

5:00

6:00

7:00

8:00

9:00

10:00

17 Friday

READ
John 14

6:00

7:00

8:00

9:00

10:00

11:00

12:00

1:00

2:00

3:00

4:00

5:00

6:00

7:00

8:00

9:00

10:00

18 Saturday

READ
John 15

6:00

7:00

8:00

9:00

10:00

11:00

12:00

1:00

2:00

3:00

4:00

5:00

6:00

7:00

8:00

9:00

10:00

What are your prayer priorities this week?

To Do

Things you're thankful for this week:

JUNE 19 – JUNE 25

19 Sunday	*20 Monday*	*21 Tuesday*	*22 Wednesday*
READ *Luke 19*	READ *Ezekiel 36*	READ *Philemon 1*	READ *Romans 10*
6:00	6:00	6:00	6:00
7:00	7:00	7:00	7:00
8:00	8:00	8:00	8:00
9:00	9:00	9:00	9:00
10:00	10:00	10:00	10:00
11:00	11:00	11:00	11:00
12:00	12:00	12:00	12:00
1:00	1:00	1:00	1:00
2:00	2:00	2:00	2:00
3:00	3:00	3:00	3:00
4:00	4:00	4:00	4:00
5:00	5:00	5:00	5:00
6:00	6:00	6:00	6:00
7:00	7:00	7:00	7:00
8:00	8:00	8:00	8:00
9:00	9:00	9:00	9:00
10:00	10:00	10:00	10:00

You're lifted above. When the muck of life starts pulling you down like quicksand, I will rescue you. I will lift you up to where I live, above the mire where the air is clean and the breeze is fresh.

Love, Jesus

Ephesians 2:6

23 Thursday

READ
Romans 12

6:00

7:00

8:00

9:00

10:00

11:00

12:00

1:00

2:00

3:00

4:00

5:00

6:00

7:00

8:00

9:00

10:00

24 Friday

READ
2 Corinthians 12

6:00

7:00

8:00

9:00

10:00

11:00

12:00

1:00

2:00

3:00

4:00

5:00

6:00

7:00

8:00

9:00

10:00

25 Saturday

READ
Ephesians 1

6:00

7:00

8:00

9:00

10:00

11:00

12:00

1:00

2:00

3:00

4:00

5:00

6:00

7:00

8:00

9:00

10:00

What are your prayer priorities this week?

To Do

Things you're thankful for this week:

JUNE 26 – JULY 2

26 *Sunday*	27 *Monday*	28 *Tuesday*	29 *Wednesday*
READ	READ	READ	READ
Ephesians 2	*Ephesians 3*	*Ephesians 4*	*Ephesians 5*
6:00	6:00	6:00	6:00
7:00	7:00	7:00	7:00
8:00	8:00	8:00	8:00
9:00	9:00	9:00	9:00
10:00	10:00	10:00	10:00
11:00	11:00	11:00	11:00
12:00	12:00	12:00	12:00
1:00	1:00	1:00	1:00
2:00	2:00	2:00	2:00
3:00	3:00	3:00	3:00
4:00	4:00	4:00	4:00
5:00	5:00	5:00	5:00
6:00	6:00	6:00	6:00
7:00	7:00	7:00	7:00
8:00	8:00	8:00	8:00
9:00	9:00	9:00	9:00
10:00	10:00	10:00	10:00

You receive my grace. I know you'd like to help—that you'd feel better if you could chip in or work it off or carry some of your own weight. Sorry. I've got it covered. My grace is a gift, and there's nothing you can do to earn it. Just receive it with a thankful heart.

Love, Jesus

Ephesians 2:8

30 Thursday

READ
Ephesians 6

6:00

7:00

8:00

9:00

10:00

11:00

12:00

1:00

2:00

3:00

4:00

5:00

6:00

7:00

8:00

9:00

10:00

1 Friday

READ
Genesis 15

6:00

7:00

8:00

9:00

10:00

11:00

12:00

1:00

2:00

3:00

4:00

5:00

6:00

7:00

8:00

9:00

10:00

2 Saturday

READ
Genesis 44

6:00

7:00

8:00

9:00

10:00

11:00

12:00

1:00

2:00

3:00

4:00

5:00

6:00

7:00

8:00

9:00

10:00

What are your prayer priorities this week?

To Do

Things you're thankful for this week:

Review your gratitude notes from previous weeks, and write a prayer to Jesus thanking him for this month.

What experiences, insights, and moments helped keep Jesus a priority in your life in June? Record them here so you don't forget them.

Reviewing the previous month, how did focusing on the right priorities make a difference in your life?

Are there any ways you might adjust your priorities in the month ahead?

Review your appointments and tasks for the coming month. In what ways are they helping you focus on Jesus' priority of loving others? Is there anything you need to cancel, add, or change? Pray about it; then update your schedule as needed.

Now write a prayer thanking Jesus for new opportunities coming in July, and include one way you're planning to stay focused on him.

Setting Jesus-Centered Priorities, Third Quarter

Look to Jesus' example to guide your life's priorities.

Before committing to naming your priorities, spend five to 10 minutes writing or mapping a sketch of everything that's currently most important to you in your life. Don't edit yourself; it's okay if this list includes your most personal desires—good, bad, or otherwise. Be open and honest with yourself about where your heart is right now.

Now think about Jesus' top priority: loving others. How is Jesus' command connected to the most important things in your life? Pray about it. Challenge yourself to be open to what that really means for you. If being centered on Jesus is all about loving others, how will that affect your priorities? Make a list of your life's priorities here.

With Jesus' command in mind, prayerfully consider your top priority—what's the most important investment of your time and energy—for you to focus on for the next three months. Your priority can be anything: your family, job, friends, special project—whichever part of your life you want to be more centered on Jesus.

3RD QUARTER PRIORITY (JULY, AUGUST, SEPTEMBER)

Focusing on this priority is important to *you* because…

Focusing on this priority is important to *Jesus* because…

ACTION STEPS needed to stay focused…

If you've identified one or two other top priorities, write them here along with the reasons they're important and what you plan to do to keep them in focus.

To Do

JULY 2022

Sunday	Monday	Tuesday
26	27	28
3	4 Independence Day	5
10	11	12
17	18	19
24	25	26

Notes

This month, keep your priorities focused on Jesus by...

Wednesday	Thursday	Friday	Saturday
29	30	1	2
6	7	8	9
13	14	15	16
20	21	22	23
27	28	29	30

Loving others: Loving others must always show up in your priorities.
Who are you going to show love to this month? Write one to three names
here, and schedule time to reach out to those people.

JULY 3 – JULY 9

3 Sunday

READ
Exodus 1

6:00

7:00

8:00

9:00

10:00

11:00

12:00

1:00

2:00

3:00

4:00

5:00

6:00

7:00

8:00

9:00

10:00

4 Monday

READ
Exodus 2

6:00

7:00

8:00

9:00

10:00

11:00

12:00

1:00

2:00

3:00

4:00

5:00

6:00

7:00

8:00

9:00

10:00

5 Tuesday

READ
Exodus 3

6:00

7:00

8:00

9:00

10:00

11:00

12:00

1:00

2:00

3:00

4:00

5:00

6:00

7:00

8:00

9:00

10:00

6 Wednesday

READ
Exodus 12

6:00

7:00

8:00

9:00

10:00

11:00

12:00

1:00

2:00

3:00

4:00

5:00

6:00

7:00

8:00

9:00

10:00

You're my work. You're so busy working that it's easy to think I'm one more thing to do. But I do not need your works. Instead, you're *my* work, and I love my work. Let's labor together for love and sacrifice and the good fight.

Love, Jesus

Ephesians 2:10

7 Thursday

READ
Exodus 14

6:00

7:00

8:00

9:00

10:00

11:00

12:00

1:00

2:00

3:00

4:00

5:00

6:00

7:00

8:00

9:00

10:00

8 Friday

READ
Exodus 19

6:00

7:00

8:00

9:00

10:00

11:00

12:00

1:00

2:00

3:00

4:00

5:00

6:00

7:00

8:00

9:00

10:00

9 Saturday

READ
Exodus 20

6:00

7:00

8:00

9:00

10:00

11:00

12:00

1:00

2:00

3:00

4:00

5:00

6:00

7:00

8:00

9:00

10:00

What are your prayer priorities this week?

....

....

....

....

....

....

....

....

....

To Do

....

....

....

....

....

....

....

....

....

Things you're thankful for this week:

10 Sunday
READ
Leviticus 4

6:00
7:00
8:00
9:00
10:00
11:00
12:00
1:00
2:00
3:00
4:00
5:00
6:00
7:00
8:00
9:00
10:00

11 Monday
READ
Leviticus 19

6:00
7:00
8:00
9:00
10:00
11:00
12:00
1:00
2:00
3:00
4:00
5:00
6:00
7:00
8:00
9:00
10:00

12 Tuesday
READ
Numbers 9

6:00
7:00
8:00
9:00
10:00
11:00
12:00
1:00
2:00
3:00
4:00
5:00
6:00
7:00
8:00
9:00
10:00

13 Wednesday
READ
Deuteronomy 5

6:00
7:00
8:00
9:00
10:00
11:00
12:00
1:00
2:00
3:00
4:00
5:00
6:00
7:00
8:00
9:00
10:00

You're confident. I can see you holding back, timidly hiding your thoughts and emotions from me. I haven't asked you to do this—to edit and censor yourself. I want you to be confident, to be bold, to be daring. Take the risk of being yourself.

Love, Jesus

Ephesians 3:12

14 Thursday

READ
Deuteronomy 6

6:00

7:00

8:00

9:00

10:00

11:00

12:00

1:00

2:00

3:00

4:00

5:00

6:00

7:00

8:00

9:00

10:00

15 Friday

READ
Deuteronomy 34

6:00

7:00

8:00

9:00

10:00

11:00

12:00

1:00

2:00

3:00

4:00

5:00

6:00

7:00

8:00

9:00

10:00

16 Saturday

READ
Joshua 1

6:00

7:00

8:00

9:00

10:00

11:00

12:00

1:00

2:00

3:00

4:00

5:00

6:00

7:00

8:00

9:00

10:00

What are your prayer priorities this week?

To Do

Things you're thankful for this week:

JULY 17 – JULY 23

17 Sunday

READ
Joshua 2

6:00

7:00

8:00

9:00

10:00

11:00

12:00

1:00

2:00

3:00

4:00

5:00

6:00

7:00

8:00

9:00

10:00

18 Monday

READ
Joshua 3

6:00

7:00

8:00

9:00

10:00

11:00

12:00

1:00

2:00

3:00

4:00

5:00

6:00

7:00

8:00

9:00

10:00

19 Tuesday

READ
Judges 2

6:00

7:00

8:00

9:00

10:00

11:00

12:00

1:00

2:00

3:00

4:00

5:00

6:00

7:00

8:00

9:00

10:00

20 Wednesday

READ
Ruth 1

6:00

7:00

8:00

9:00

10:00

11:00

12:00

1:00

2:00

3:00

4:00

5:00

6:00

7:00

8:00

9:00

10:00

You will not be moved. When you feel like your feet are slipping, remember this: I will keep you grounded. I'm standing behind you, holding you up. I'm at your feet, pressing your soles to the ground. You will not be moved.

Love, Jesus

Ephesians 3:17

21 Thursday

READ
Ruth 2

6:00

7:00

8:00

9:00

10:00

11:00

12:00

1:00

2:00

3:00

4:00

5:00

6:00

7:00

8:00

9:00

10:00

22 Friday

READ
Ruth 3

6:00

7:00

8:00

9:00

10:00

11:00

12:00

1:00

2:00

3:00

4:00

5:00

6:00

7:00

8:00

9:00

10:00

23 Saturday

READ
Ruth 4

6:00

7:00

8:00

9:00

10:00

11:00

12:00

1:00

2:00

3:00

4:00

5:00

6:00

7:00

8:00

9:00

10:00

What are your prayer priorities this week?

To Do

Things you're thankful for this week:

JULY 24 – JULY 30

24 Sunday	25 Monday	26 Tuesday	27 Wednesday
READ 1 Samuel 1	READ 1 Samuel 3	READ 1 Samuel 16	READ 1 Samuel 17
6:00	6:00	6:00	6:00
7:00	7:00	7:00	7:00
8:00	8:00	8:00	8:00
9:00	9:00	9:00	9:00
10:00	10:00	10:00	10:00
11:00	11:00	11:00	11:00
12:00	12:00	12:00	12:00
1:00	1:00	1:00	1:00
2:00	2:00	2:00	2:00
3:00	3:00	3:00	3:00
4:00	4:00	4:00	4:00
5:00	5:00	5:00	5:00
6:00	6:00	6:00	6:00
7:00	7:00	7:00	7:00
8:00	8:00	8:00	8:00
9:00	9:00	9:00	9:00
10:00	10:00	10:00	10:00

You have everything you need. Your true needs are not what you think. You want smooth, happy, plenty. But I know that bumpy, weak, and lacking is better for you because *they* are my refiner's fire. I'll choose your holiness over your happiness every time, for it is precious to me.

Love, Jesus

Philippians 4:19

28 Thursday	29 Friday	30 Saturday	*What are your prayer priorities this week?*
READ *2 Samuel 7*	READ *2 Samuel 12*	READ *1 Kings 9*	
6:00	6:00	6:00	
7:00	7:00	7:00	
8:00	8:00	8:00	
9:00	9:00	9:00	
10:00	10:00	10:00	
11:00	11:00	11:00	
12:00	12:00	12:00	
1:00	1:00	1:00	
2:00	2:00	2:00	
3:00	3:00	3:00	*To Do*
4:00	4:00	4:00	
5:00	5:00	5:00	
6:00	6:00	6:00	
7:00	7:00	7:00	
8:00	8:00	8:00	
9:00	9:00	9:00	
10:00	10:00	10:00	

Things you're thankful for this week:

Review your gratitude notes from previous weeks, and write a prayer to Jesus thanking him for this month.

What experiences, insights, and moments helped keep Jesus a priority in your life in July? Record them here so you don't forget them.

Reviewing the previous month, how did focusing on the right priorities make a difference in your life?

Are there any ways you might adjust your priorities in the month ahead?

Review your appointments and tasks for the coming month. In what ways are they helping you focus on Jesus' priority of loving others? Is there anything you need to cancel, add, or change? Pray about it; then update your schedule as needed.

Now write a prayer thanking Jesus for new opportunities coming in August, and include one way you're planning to stay focused on him.

AUGUST 2022

Sunday	Monday	Tuesday
31	1	2
7	8	9
14	15	16
21	22	23
28	29	30

Notes

This month, keep your priorities focused on Jesus by...

Wednesday	Thursday	Friday	Saturday
3	4	5	6
10	11	12	13
17	18	19	20
24	25	26	27
31	1	2	3

Loving others: Loving others must always show up in your priorities.
Who are you going to show love to this month? Write one to three names
here, and schedule time to reach out to those people.

31 Sunday

READ
1 Kings 19

6:00

7:00

8:00

9:00

10:00

11:00

12:00

1:00

2:00

3:00

4:00

5:00

6:00

7:00

8:00

9:00

10:00

1 Monday

READ
2 Kings 5

6:00

7:00

8:00

9:00

10:00

11:00

12:00

1:00

2:00

3:00

4:00

5:00

6:00

7:00

8:00

9:00

10:00

2 Tuesday

READ
2 Kings 25

6:00

7:00

8:00

9:00

10:00

11:00

12:00

1:00

2:00

3:00

4:00

5:00

6:00

7:00

8:00

9:00

10:00

3 Wednesday

READ
1 Chronicles 17

6:00

7:00

8:00

9:00

10:00

11:00

12:00

1:00

2:00

3:00

4:00

5:00

6:00

7:00

8:00

9:00

10:00

You're protected. It's difficult to understand why I expose you to pain—why I do not intervene. But here's what you don't see: I'm always guarding your heart and your mind, and *nothing*—not even death—can climb over my wall of protection to steal your joy and peace.

Love, Jesus

Philippians 4:7

4 Thursday	5 Friday	6 Saturday	What are your prayer priorities this week?
READ	READ	READ	
2 Chronicles 30	*Ezra 3*	*Nehemiah 1*	
6:00	6:00	6:00	
7:00	7:00	7:00	
8:00	8:00	8:00	
9:00	9:00	9:00	
10:00	10:00	10:00	
11:00	11:00	11:00	
12:00	12:00	12:00	
1:00	1:00	1:00	
2:00	2:00	2:00	
3:00	3:00	3:00	*To Do*
4:00	4:00	4:00	
5:00	5:00	5:00	
6:00	6:00	6:00	
7:00	7:00	7:00	
8:00	8:00	8:00	
9:00	9:00	9:00	
10:00	10:00	10:00	

Things you're thankful for this week:

7 Sunday	8 Monday	9 Tuesday	10 Wednesday
READ	READ	READ	READ
Esther 4	*Job 31*	*Job 38*	*Job 39*
6:00	6:00	6:00	6:00
7:00	7:00	7:00	7:00
8:00	8:00	8:00	8:00
9:00	9:00	9:00	9:00
10:00	10:00	10:00	10:00
11:00	11:00	11:00	11:00
12:00	12:00	12:00	12:00
1:00	1:00	1:00	1:00
2:00	2:00	2:00	2:00
3:00	3:00	3:00	3:00
4:00	4:00	4:00	4:00
5:00	5:00	5:00	5:00
6:00	6:00	6:00	6:00
7:00	7:00	7:00	7:00
8:00	8:00	8:00	8:00
9:00	9:00	9:00	9:00
10:00	10:00	10:00	10:00

You're a Kingdom-bearer. My kingdom is different from the ones you're used to. It embraces instead of divides, serves instead of promotes, forgives instead of harms. And because I'm in you, you're bringing my kingdom to the *here* and *now*. Let it expand and influence, converting darkness into light.

Love, Jesus

Philippians 3:20

11 Thursday

READ
Job 40

6:00

7:00

8:00

9:00

10:00

11:00

12:00

1:00

2:00

3:00

4:00

5:00

6:00

7:00

8:00

9:00

10:00

12 Friday

READ
Job 42

6:00

7:00

8:00

9:00

10:00

11:00

12:00

1:00

2:00

3:00

4:00

5:00

6:00

7:00

8:00

9:00

10:00

13 Saturday

READ
Proverbs 1

6:00

7:00

8:00

9:00

10:00

11:00

12:00

1:00

2:00

3:00

4:00

5:00

6:00

7:00

8:00

9:00

10:00

What are your prayer priorities this week?

To Do

Things you're thankful for this week:

14 Sunday

READ
Proverbs 2

6:00

7:00

8:00

9:00

10:00

11:00

12:00

1:00

2:00

3:00

4:00

5:00

6:00

7:00

8:00

9:00

10:00

15 Monday

READ
Proverbs 3

6:00

7:00

8:00

9:00

10:00

11:00

12:00

1:00

2:00

3:00

4:00

5:00

6:00

7:00

8:00

9:00

10:00

16 Tuesday

READ
Ecclesiastes 1

6:00

7:00

8:00

9:00

10:00

11:00

12:00

1:00

2:00

3:00

4:00

5:00

6:00

7:00

8:00

9:00

10:00

17 Wednesday

READ
Song of Songs 1

6:00

7:00

8:00

9:00

10:00

11:00

12:00

1:00

2:00

3:00

4:00

5:00

6:00

7:00

8:00

9:00

10:00

You're hidden away. You should know that I'm not the sharing type. Now that you're mine, I'm hiding you away, beyond the reach of the enemy's supernatural powers. Though he covets you for his purposes, you've been set aside for *my* purpose, and my hiding place is secure.

Love, Jesus

Colossians 3:3

18 Thursday

READ
Isaiah 1

6:00

7:00

8:00

9:00

10:00

11:00

12:00

1:00

2:00

3:00

4:00

5:00

6:00

7:00

8:00

9:00

10:00

19 Friday

READ
Isaiah 2

6:00

7:00

8:00

9:00

10:00

11:00

12:00

1:00

2:00

3:00

4:00

5:00

6:00

7:00

8:00

9:00

10:00

20 Saturday

READ
Isaiah 55

6:00

7:00

8:00

9:00

10:00

11:00

12:00

1:00

2:00

3:00

4:00

5:00

6:00

7:00

8:00

9:00

10:00

What are your prayer priorities this week?

To Do

Things you're thankful for this week:

AUG 21 – AUG 27

21 Sunday	*22 Monday*	*23 Tuesday*	*24 Wednesday*
READ	READ	READ	READ
Lamentations 3	*Ezekiel 34*	*Hosea 2*	*Joel 2*
6:00	6:00	6:00	6:00
7:00	7:00	7:00	7:00
8:00	8:00	8:00	8:00
9:00	9:00	9:00	9:00
10:00	10:00	10:00	10:00
11:00	11:00	11:00	11:00
12:00	12:00	12:00	12:00
1:00	1:00	1:00	1:00
2:00	2:00	2:00	2:00
3:00	3:00	3:00	3:00
4:00	4:00	4:00	4:00
5:00	5:00	5:00	5:00
6:00	6:00	6:00	6:00
7:00	7:00	7:00	7:00
8:00	8:00	8:00	8:00
9:00	9:00	9:00	9:00
10:00	10:00	10:00	10:00

Your life is mine. "Busy." "A work in progress." "All right." You often describe your life with words like these. But I have a new description of you: Me. It seems like a strange way to describe your life, but after you said yes to my salvation, your life was traded for mine. Now I'm the word that matters most.

Love, Jesus

Colossians 3:4

25 Thursday

READ
Amos 9

6:00

7:00

8:00

9:00

10:00

11:00

12:00

1:00

2:00

3:00

4:00

5:00

6:00

7:00

8:00

9:00

10:00

26 Friday

READ
Obadiah 1

6:00

7:00

8:00

9:00

10:00

11:00

12:00

1:00

2:00

3:00

4:00

5:00

6:00

7:00

8:00

9:00

10:00

27 Saturday

READ
Nahum 1

6:00

7:00

8:00

9:00

10:00

11:00

12:00

1:00

2:00

3:00

4:00

5:00

6:00

7:00

8:00

9:00

10:00

What are your prayer priorities this week?

To Do

Things you're thankful for this week:

28 Sunday

READ
Habakkuk 1

6:00

7:00

8:00

9:00

10:00

11:00

12:00

1:00

2:00

3:00

4:00

5:00

6:00

7:00

8:00

9:00

10:00

29 Monday

READ
Zephaniah 3

6:00

7:00

8:00

9:00

10:00

11:00

12:00

1:00

2:00

3:00

4:00

5:00

6:00

7:00

8:00

9:00

10:00

30 Tuesday

READ
Haggai 2

6:00

7:00

8:00

9:00

10:00

11:00

12:00

1:00

2:00

3:00

4:00

5:00

6:00

7:00

8:00

9:00

10:00

31 Wednesday

READ
Malachi 3

6:00

7:00

8:00

9:00

10:00

11:00

12:00

1:00

2:00

3:00

4:00

5:00

6:00

7:00

8:00

9:00

10:00

You're chosen. For all the lonely times you were left out, passed over, left behind, I have this to say: You're chosen by me, picked and set aside. You're now my insider, bearing my mark, never alone again.

Love, Jesus

Colossians 3:12

1 Thursday	2 Friday	3 Saturday	*What are your prayer priorities this week?*
READ	READ	READ	
John 7	*John 8*	*John 9*	
6:00	6:00	6:00	
7:00	7:00	7:00	
8:00	8:00	8:00	
9:00	9:00	9:00	
10:00	10:00	10:00	
11:00	11:00	11:00	
12:00	12:00	12:00	
1:00	1:00	1:00	
2:00	2:00	2:00	
3:00	3:00	3:00	*To Do*
4:00	4:00	4:00	
5:00	5:00	5:00	
6:00	6:00	6:00	
7:00	7:00	7:00	
8:00	8:00	8:00	
9:00	9:00	9:00	
10:00	10:00	10:00	

Things you're thankful for this week:

Review your gratitude notes from previous weeks, and write a prayer to Jesus thanking him for this month.

What experiences, insights, and moments helped keep Jesus a priority in your life in August? Record them here so you don't forget them.

Reviewing the previous month, how did focusing on the right priorities make a difference in your life?

Are there any ways you might adjust your priorities in the month ahead?

Review your appointments and tasks for the coming month. In what ways are they helping you focus on Jesus' priority of loving others? Is there anything you need to cancel, add, or change? Pray about it; then update your schedule as needed.

Now write a prayer thanking Jesus for new opportunities coming in September, and include one way you're planning to stay focused on him.

SEPTEMBER 2022

To Do

Notes

Sunday	Monday	Tuesday
28	29	30
4	5 Labor Day	6
11	12	13
18	19	20
25	26	27

This month, keep your priorities focused on Jesus by...

Wednesday	Thursday	Friday	Saturday
31	1	2	3
7	8	9	10
14	15	16	17
21	22	23	24
28	29	30	1

Loving others: Loving others must always show up in your priorities. Who are you going to show love to this month? Write one to three names here, and schedule time to reach out to those people.

4 *Sunday*	5 *Monday*	6 *Tuesday*	7 *Wednesday*
READ	READ	READ	READ
John 10	*John 16*	*John 17*	*Matthew 11*
6:00	6:00	6:00	6:00
7:00	7:00	7:00	7:00
8:00	8:00	8:00	8:00
9:00	9:00	9:00	9:00
10:00	10:00	10:00	10:00
11:00	11:00	11:00	11:00
12:00	12:00	12:00	12:00
1:00	1:00	1:00	1:00
2:00	2:00	2:00	2:00
3:00	3:00	3:00	3:00
4:00	4:00	4:00	4:00
5:00	5:00	5:00	5:00
6:00	6:00	6:00	6:00
7:00	7:00	7:00	7:00
8:00	8:00	8:00	8:00
9:00	9:00	9:00	9:00
10:00	10:00	10:00	10:00

You're my messenger. You're my messenger to a lost and hurting world. Don't be so busy or distracted that you speak rashly; instead, let me speak life through you. Speak it boldly, speak it often. And believe that speaking it will accomplish my purpose.

Love, Jesus

1 Thessalonians 2:4

8 Thursday

READ
Isaiah 40

6:00

7:00

8:00

9:00

10:00

11:00

12:00

1:00

2:00

3:00

4:00

5:00

6:00

7:00

8:00

9:00

10:00

9 Friday

READ
Hebrews 1

6:00

7:00

8:00

9:00

10:00

11:00

12:00

1:00

2:00

3:00

4:00

5:00

6:00

7:00

8:00

9:00

10:00

10 Saturday

READ
Hebrews 2

6:00

7:00

8:00

9:00

10:00

11:00

12:00

1:00

2:00

3:00

4:00

5:00

6:00

7:00

8:00

9:00

10:00

What are your prayer priorities this week?

To Do

Things you're thankful for this week:

11 Sunday
READ
Hebrews 3

6:00

7:00

8:00

9:00

10:00

11:00

12:00

1:00

2:00

3:00

4:00

5:00

6:00

7:00

8:00

9:00

10:00

12 Monday
READ
Hebrews 4

6:00

7:00

8:00

9:00

10:00

11:00

12:00

1:00

2:00

3:00

4:00

5:00

6:00

7:00

8:00

9:00

10:00

13 Tuesday
READ
Hebrews 5

6:00

7:00

8:00

9:00

10:00

11:00

12:00

1:00

2:00

3:00

4:00

5:00

6:00

7:00

8:00

9:00

10:00

14 Wednesday
READ
Hebrews 6

6:00

7:00

8:00

9:00

10:00

11:00

12:00

1:00

2:00

3:00

4:00

5:00

6:00

7:00

8:00

9:00

10:00

You please me. Though your natural way—your *old* way—seeks approval from others, I have set you free from their hold over you. You were not meant to be a people-pleaser, boxed into their expectations and whims. You please me. Period. My approval is all you need.

Love, Jesus

1 Thessalonians 2:4

15 Thursday

READ
Hebrews 7

6:00

7:00

8:00

9:00

10:00

11:00

12:00

1:00

2:00

3:00

4:00

5:00

6:00

7:00

8:00

9:00

10:00

16 Friday

READ
Genesis 14

6:00

7:00

8:00

9:00

10:00

11:00

12:00

1:00

2:00

3:00

4:00

5:00

6:00

7:00

8:00

9:00

10:00

17 Saturday

READ
Hebrews 8

6:00

7:00

8:00

9:00

10:00

11:00

12:00

1:00

2:00

3:00

4:00

5:00

6:00

7:00

8:00

9:00

10:00

What are your prayer priorities this week?

To Do

Things you're thankful for this week:

18 Sunday	19 Monday	20 Tuesday	21 Wednesday
READ	READ	READ	READ
Hebrews 9	*Hebrews 10*	*Isaiah 42*	*Isaiah 43*
6:00	6:00	6:00	6:00
7:00	7:00	7:00	7:00
8:00	8:00	8:00	8:00
9:00	9:00	9:00	9:00
10:00	10:00	10:00	10:00
11:00	11:00	11:00	11:00
12:00	12:00	12:00	12:00
1:00	1:00	1:00	1:00
2:00	2:00	2:00	2:00
3:00	3:00	3:00	3:00
4:00	4:00	4:00	4:00
5:00	5:00	5:00	5:00
6:00	6:00	6:00	6:00
7:00	7:00	7:00	7:00
8:00	8:00	8:00	8:00
9:00	9:00	9:00	9:00
10:00	10:00	10:00	10:00

You're truth. Here's the truth about truth: It's not a moving target; it's not popular opinion; it's not majority wins. I am Truth, and because I am in you, you and the rest of my followers are also truth. When you follow my example by loving, serving, and healing, you're pillars of truth, stabilizing this world.

Love, Jesus

1 Timothy 3:15

22 Thursday	23 Friday	24 Saturday	What are your prayer priorities this week?
READ *2 Samuel 22*	READ *Philippians 1*	READ *Philippians 2*	
6:00	6:00	6:00	
7:00	7:00	7:00	
8:00	8:00	8:00	
9:00	9:00	9:00	
10:00	10:00	10:00	
11:00	11:00	11:00	
12:00	12:00	12:00	
1:00	1:00	1:00	
2:00	2:00	2:00	
3:00	3:00	3:00	*To Do*
4:00	4:00	4:00	
5:00	5:00	5:00	
6:00	6:00	6:00	
7:00	7:00	7:00	
8:00	8:00	8:00	
9:00	9:00	9:00	
10:00	10:00	10:00	

Things you're thankful for this week:

25 Sunday

READ
Philippians 3

| 6:00 |
| 7:00 |
| 8:00 |
| 9:00 |
| 10:00 |
| 11:00 |
| 12:00 |
| 1:00 |
| 2:00 |
| 3:00 |
| 4:00 |
| 5:00 |
| 6:00 |
| 7:00 |
| 8:00 |
| 9:00 |
| 10:00 |

26 Monday

READ
Philippians 4

| 6:00 |
| 7:00 |
| 8:00 |
| 9:00 |
| 10:00 |
| 11:00 |
| 12:00 |
| 1:00 |
| 2:00 |
| 3:00 |
| 4:00 |
| 5:00 |
| 6:00 |
| 7:00 |
| 8:00 |
| 9:00 |
| 10:00 |

27 Tuesday

READ
Colossians 1

| 6:00 |
| 7:00 |
| 8:00 |
| 9:00 |
| 10:00 |
| 11:00 |
| 12:00 |
| 1:00 |
| 2:00 |
| 3:00 |
| 4:00 |
| 5:00 |
| 6:00 |
| 7:00 |
| 8:00 |
| 9:00 |
| 10:00 |

28 Wednesday

READ
Colossians 2

| 6:00 |
| 7:00 |
| 8:00 |
| 9:00 |
| 10:00 |
| 11:00 |
| 12:00 |
| 1:00 |
| 2:00 |
| 3:00 |
| 4:00 |
| 5:00 |
| 6:00 |
| 7:00 |
| 8:00 |
| 9:00 |
| 10:00 |

You're focused on what matters most. Your thoughts frequently buzz around like frenzied bees in a hive. Some offer a sweet nectar, but others offend with a sting. If you'll let me, I can transform this frenzy into a calm, harmonized hum by directing each thought toward one focal point: Me.

Love, Jesus

Hebrews 3:1

29 Thursday	30 Friday	1 Saturday
READ	READ	READ
Colossians 3	*Colossians 4*	*Psalm 1*
6:00	6:00	6:00
7:00	7:00	7:00
8:00	8:00	8:00
9:00	9:00	9:00
10:00	10:00	10:00
11:00	11:00	11:00
12:00	12:00	12:00
1:00	1:00	1:00
2:00	2:00	2:00
3:00	3:00	3:00
4:00	4:00	4:00
5:00	5:00	5:00
6:00	6:00	6:00
7:00	7:00	7:00
8:00	8:00	8:00
9:00	9:00	9:00
10:00	10:00	10:00

What are your prayer priorities this week?

To Do

Things you're thankful for this week:

Review your gratitude notes from previous weeks, and write a prayer to Jesus thanking him for this month.

What experiences, insights, and moments helped keep Jesus a priority in your life in September? Record them here so you don't forget them.

Reviewing the previous month, how did focusing on the right priorities make a difference in your life?

Are there any ways you might adjust your priorities in the month ahead?

Review your appointments and tasks for the coming month. In what ways are they helping you focus on Jesus' priority of loving others? Is there anything you need to cancel, add, or change? Pray about it; then update your schedule as needed.

Now write a prayer thanking Jesus for new opportunities coming in October, and include one way you're planning to stay focused on him.

Setting Jesus-Centered Priorities, Fourth Quarter

Finish the year strong by looking to Jesus to guide your priorities.

Before committing to naming your priorities, spend five to 10 minutes writing or mapping a sketch of everything that's currently most important to you in your life. Don't edit yourself; it's okay if this list includes your most personal desires—good, bad, or otherwise. Be open and honest with yourself about where your heart is right now.

Now think about Jesus' top priority: loving others. How is Jesus' command connected to the most important things in your life? Pray about it. Challenge yourself to be open to what that really means for you. If being centered on Jesus is all about loving others, how will that affect your priorities? Make a list of your life's priorities here.

With Jesus' command in mind, prayerfully consider your top priority—what's the most important investment of your time and energy—for you to focus on for the next three months. Your priority can be anything: your family, job, friends, special project—whichever part of your life you want to be more centered on Jesus.

4TH QUARTER PRIORITY (OCTOBER, NOVEMBER, DECEMBER)

Focusing on this priority is important to *you* because…

Focusing on this priority is important to *Jesus* because…

ACTION STEPS needed to stay focused…

If you've identified one or two other top priorities, write them here along with the reasons they're important and what you plan to do to keep them in focus.

To Do

Sunday	Monday	Tuesday
25	26	27
2	3	4
9	10	11
16	17	18
23	24	25
30	31 Halloween	1

Notes

This month, keep your priorities focused on Jesus by...

Wednesday	Thursday	Friday	Saturday
28	29	30	1
5	6	7	8
12	13	14	15
19	20	21	22
26	27	28	29
2	3	4	5

Loving others: Loving others must always show up in your priorities. Who are you going to focus on loving this month? Write one to three names here, and schedule time to reach out to those people.

2 Sunday

READ
Psalm 2

6:00

7:00

8:00

9:00

10:00

11:00

12:00

1:00

2:00

3:00

4:00

5:00

6:00

7:00

8:00

9:00

10:00

3 Monday

READ
Psalm 23

6:00

7:00

8:00

9:00

10:00

11:00

12:00

1:00

2:00

3:00

4:00

5:00

6:00

7:00

8:00

9:00

10:00

4 Tuesday

READ
Psalm 25

6:00

7:00

8:00

9:00

10:00

11:00

12:00

1:00

2:00

3:00

4:00

5:00

6:00

7:00

8:00

9:00

10:00

5 Wednesday

READ
Psalm 27

6:00

7:00

8:00

9:00

10:00

11:00

12:00

1:00

2:00

3:00

4:00

5:00

6:00

7:00

8:00

9:00

10:00

You're resistant (in a good way). I'm proud that you don't make a habit of sinning. You avoid temptation; you don't linger in bad places; you withhold judgment and sharp words. This resistance is challenging, but I'm by your side, helping you triumph.

Love, Jesus

1 John 5:18

6 Thursday

READ
Psalm 34

6:00

7:00

8:00

9:00

10:00

11:00

12:00

1:00

2:00

3:00

4:00

5:00

6:00

7:00

8:00

9:00

10:00

7 Friday

READ
Psalm 38

6:00

7:00

8:00

9:00

10:00

11:00

12:00

1:00

2:00

3:00

4:00

5:00

6:00

7:00

8:00

9:00

10:00

8 Saturday

READ
Psalm 40

6:00

7:00

8:00

9:00

10:00

11:00

12:00

1:00

2:00

3:00

4:00

5:00

6:00

7:00

8:00

9:00

10:00

What are your prayer priorities this week?

To Do

Things you're thankful for this week:

9 Sunday

READ
Psalm 69

6:00

7:00

8:00

9:00

10:00

11:00

12:00

1:00

2:00

3:00

4:00

5:00

6:00

7:00

8:00

9:00

10:00

10 Monday

READ
Psalm 90

6:00

7:00

8:00

9:00

10:00

11:00

12:00

1:00

2:00

3:00

4:00

5:00

6:00

7:00

8:00

9:00

10:00

11 Tuesday

READ
Psalm 93

6:00

7:00

8:00

9:00

10:00

11:00

12:00

1:00

2:00

3:00

4:00

5:00

6:00

7:00

8:00

9:00

10:00

12 Wednesday

READ
Psalm 100

6:00

7:00

8:00

9:00

10:00

11:00

12:00

1:00

2:00

3:00

4:00

5:00

6:00

7:00

8:00

9:00

10:00

You belong. You don't have to be on your own, because you belong to me. You're a treasured part of a forever family that won't break up—ever. We'll get through hard times, celebrate good times, and look forward to forever. Together.

Love, Jesus

John 17:9-10

13 Thursday

READ
Psalm 103

6:00

7:00

8:00

9:00

10:00

11:00

12:00

1:00

2:00

3:00

4:00

5:00

6:00

7:00

8:00

9:00

10:00

14 Friday

READ
Psalm 109

6:00

7:00

8:00

9:00

10:00

11:00

12:00

1:00

2:00

3:00

4:00

5:00

6:00

7:00

8:00

9:00

10:00

15 Saturday

READ
Psalm 110

6:00

7:00

8:00

9:00

10:00

11:00

12:00

1:00

2:00

3:00

4:00

5:00

6:00

7:00

8:00

9:00

10:00

What are your prayer priorities this week?

To Do

Things you're thankful for this week:

16 Sunday

READ
Psalm 111

6:00

7:00

8:00

9:00

10:00

11:00

12:00

1:00

2:00

3:00

4:00

5:00

6:00

7:00

8:00

9:00

10:00

17 Monday

READ
Psalm 113

6:00

7:00

8:00

9:00

10:00

11:00

12:00

1:00

2:00

3:00

4:00

5:00

6:00

7:00

8:00

9:00

10:00

18 Tuesday

READ
Psalm 115

6:00

7:00

8:00

9:00

10:00

11:00

12:00

1:00

2:00

3:00

4:00

5:00

6:00

7:00

8:00

9:00

10:00

19 Wednesday

READ
Psalm 116

6:00

7:00

8:00

9:00

10:00

11:00

12:00

1:00

2:00

3:00

4:00

5:00

6:00

7:00

8:00

9:00

10:00

You're loved back. I know one-sided love hurts a lot. I'm glad you love me, and I promise you this: You never have to wonder if I love you back. In fact, I loved you first. Our love is real, and it goes both ways.

Love, Jesus

1 John 4:9-10

20 Thursday

READ
Psalm 117

6:00

7:00

8:00

9:00

10:00

11:00

12:00

1:00

2:00

3:00

4:00

5:00

6:00

7:00

8:00

9:00

10:00

21 Friday

READ
Psalm 119:1-8

6:00

7:00

8:00

9:00

10:00

11:00

12:00

1:00

2:00

3:00

4:00

5:00

6:00

7:00

8:00

9:00

10:00

22 Saturday

READ
Psalm 119:89-96

6:00

7:00

8:00

9:00

10:00

11:00

12:00

1:00

2:00

3:00

4:00

5:00

6:00

7:00

8:00

9:00

10:00

What are your prayer priorities this week?

To Do

Things you're thankful for this week:

23 Sunday	*24 Monday*	*25 Tuesday*	*26 Wednesday*
READ	READ	READ	READ
Psalm 119:97-104	*Psalm 119:105-112*	*Psalm 130*	*Psalm 132*
6:00	6:00	6:00	6:00
7:00	7:00	7:00	7:00
8:00	8:00	8:00	8:00
9:00	9:00	9:00	9:00
10:00	10:00	10:00	10:00
11:00	11:00	11:00	11:00
12:00	12:00	12:00	12:00
1:00	1:00	1:00	1:00
2:00	2:00	2:00	2:00
3:00	3:00	3:00	3:00
4:00	4:00	4:00	4:00
5:00	5:00	5:00	5:00
6:00	6:00	6:00	6:00
7:00	7:00	7:00	7:00
8:00	8:00	8:00	8:00
9:00	9:00	9:00	9:00
10:00	10:00	10:00	10:00

You're my apprentice. Learning my way involves more than reading books and taking tests. It's a hands-on adventure! Trust me, I'll be right by your side for each discovery, each failure, and each lesson learned. Ready to get started? Follow me!

Love, Jesus

Matthew 4:19

27 Thursday

READ
Psalm 137

6:00

7:00

8:00

9:00

10:00

11:00

12:00

1:00

2:00

3:00

4:00

5:00

6:00

7:00

8:00

9:00

10:00

28 Friday

READ
Psalm 139

6:00

7:00

8:00

9:00

10:00

11:00

12:00

1:00

2:00

3:00

4:00

5:00

6:00

7:00

8:00

9:00

10:00

29 Saturday

READ
Psalm 140

6:00

7:00

8:00

9:00

10:00

11:00

12:00

1:00

2:00

3:00

4:00

5:00

6:00

7:00

8:00

9:00

10:00

What are your prayer priorities this week?

To Do

Things you're thankful for this week:

Review your gratitude notes from previous weeks, and write a prayer to Jesus thanking him for this month.

What experiences, insights, and moments helped keep Jesus a priority in your life in October? Record them here so you don't forget them.

Reviewing the previous month, how did focusing on the right priorities make a difference in your life?

Are there any ways you might adjust your priorities in the month ahead?

Review your appointments and tasks for the coming month. In what ways are they helping you focus on Jesus' priority of loving others? Is there anything you need to cancel, add, or change? Pray about it; then update your schedule as needed.

Now write a prayer thanking Jesus for new opportunities coming in November, and include one way you're planning to stay focused on him.

NOVEMBER 2022

To Do

Notes

Sunday	Monday	Tuesday
30	31	1
6	7	8
13	14	15
20	21	22
27	28	29

This month, keep your priorities focused on Jesus by...

Wednesday	Thursday	Friday	Saturday
2	3	4	5
9	10	11 Veterans Day	12
16	17	18	19
23	24 Thanksgiving Day	25	26
30	1	2	3

Loving others: Loving others must always show up in your priorities.
Who are you going to show love to this month? Write one to three names
here, and schedule time to reach out to those people.

30 Sunday	*31 Monday*	*1 Tuesday*	*2 Wednesday*
READ	READ	READ	READ
Psalm 141	*Psalm 148*	*Hebrews 11*	*Hebrews 12*
6:00	6:00	6:00	6:00
7:00	7:00	7:00	7:00
8:00	8:00	8:00	8:00
9:00	9:00	9:00	9:00
10:00	10:00	10:00	10:00
11:00	11:00	11:00	11:00
12:00	12:00	12:00	12:00
1:00	1:00	1:00	1:00
2:00	2:00	2:00	2:00
3:00	3:00	3:00	3:00
4:00	4:00	4:00	4:00
5:00	5:00	5:00	5:00
6:00	6:00	6:00	6:00
7:00	7:00	7:00	7:00
8:00	8:00	8:00	8:00
9:00	9:00	9:00	9:00
10:00	10:00	10:00	10:00

You reflect me. I'm the sun. You're the moon. I shine, and you soak in my light, reflecting my glory to the world around you. And it's awesome. You don't need to spark light on your own; just draw near to me and you'll shine away!

Love, Jesus

2 Corinthians 3:18

3 Thursday

READ
James 1

6:00

7:00

8:00

9:00

10:00

11:00

12:00

1:00

2:00

3:00

4:00

5:00

6:00

7:00

8:00

9:00

10:00

4 Friday

READ
James 2

6:00

7:00

8:00

9:00

10:00

11:00

12:00

1:00

2:00

3:00

4:00

5:00

6:00

7:00

8:00

9:00

10:00

5 Saturday

READ
James 3

6:00

7:00

8:00

9:00

10:00

11:00

12:00

1:00

2:00

3:00

4:00

5:00

6:00

7:00

8:00

9:00

10:00

What are your prayer priorities this week?

To Do

Things you're thankful for this week:

6 Sunday

READ
James 4

6:00

7:00

8:00

9:00

10:00

11:00

12:00

1:00

2:00

3:00

4:00

5:00

6:00

7:00

8:00

9:00

10:00

7 Monday

READ
James 5

6:00

7:00

8:00

9:00

10:00

11:00

12:00

1:00

2:00

3:00

4:00

5:00

6:00

7:00

8:00

9:00

10:00

8 Tuesday

READ
Isaiah 6

6:00

7:00

8:00

9:00

10:00

11:00

12:00

1:00

2:00

3:00

4:00

5:00

6:00

7:00

8:00

9:00

10:00

9 Wednesday

READ
Matthew 13

6:00

7:00

8:00

9:00

10:00

11:00

12:00

1:00

2:00

3:00

4:00

5:00

6:00

7:00

8:00

9:00

10:00

You produce fruit. I'm God. So I *could* make spiritual harvests magically appear. A bucket of love there. A bushel of peace here. A quart of joy everywhere! Instead, I include you in the growing process. We're in this together. I'm the vine; you're the branches. Attached to me, we'll produce life-giving fruit this world craves.

Love, Jesus

John 15:8, 16

10 Thursday

READ
Matthew 18

6:00

7:00

8:00

9:00

10:00

11:00

12:00

1:00

2:00

3:00

4:00

5:00

6:00

7:00

8:00

9:00

10:00

11 Friday

READ
Matthew 19

6:00

7:00

8:00

9:00

10:00

11:00

12:00

1:00

2:00

3:00

4:00

5:00

6:00

7:00

8:00

9:00

10:00

12 Saturday

READ
Matthew 23

6:00

7:00

8:00

9:00

10:00

11:00

12:00

1:00

2:00

3:00

4:00

5:00

6:00

7:00

8:00

9:00

10:00

What are your prayer priorities this week?

To Do

Things you're thankful for this week:

13 Sunday
READ
Matthew 25

6:00

7:00

8:00

9:00

10:00

11:00

12:00

1:00

2:00

3:00

4:00

5:00

6:00

7:00

8:00

9:00

10:00

14 Monday
READ
Luke 11

6:00

7:00

8:00

9:00

10:00

11:00

12:00

1:00

2:00

3:00

4:00

5:00

6:00

7:00

8:00

9:00

10:00

15 Tuesday
READ
Luke 12

6:00

7:00

8:00

9:00

10:00

11:00

12:00

1:00

2:00

3:00

4:00

5:00

6:00

7:00

8:00

9:00

10:00

16 Wednesday
READ
Luke 13

6:00

7:00

8:00

9:00

10:00

11:00

12:00

1:00

2:00

3:00

4:00

5:00

6:00

7:00

8:00

9:00

10:00

You're worth it. It's true; I gave up my life for you. I didn't have to. In fact, it hurt a lot. But I chose to because you're worth pursuing, worth sacrificing for. My love isn't fleeting fairy-tale fluff that'll eventually fade away. It's real love that treasures the real you.

Love, Jesus

1 John 3:16

17 Thursday

READ
Luke 14

6:00

7:00

8:00

9:00

10:00

11:00

12:00

1:00

2:00

3:00

4:00

5:00

6:00

7:00

8:00

9:00

10:00

18 Friday

READ
Luke 15

6:00

7:00

8:00

9:00

10:00

11:00

12:00

1:00

2:00

3:00

4:00

5:00

6:00

7:00

8:00

9:00

10:00

19 Saturday

READ
Luke 16

6:00

7:00

8:00

9:00

10:00

11:00

12:00

1:00

2:00

3:00

4:00

5:00

6:00

7:00

8:00

9:00

10:00

What are your prayer priorities this week?

To Do

Things you're thankful for this week:

20 Sunday
READ
Luke 17

6:00
7:00
8:00
9:00
10:00
11:00
12:00
1:00
2:00
3:00
4:00
5:00
6:00
7:00
8:00
9:00
10:00

21 Monday
READ
Luke 18

6:00
7:00
8:00
9:00
10:00
11:00
12:00
1:00
2:00
3:00
4:00
5:00
6:00
7:00
8:00
9:00
10:00

22 Tuesday
READ
Psalm 51

6:00
7:00
8:00
9:00
10:00
11:00
12:00
1:00
2:00
3:00
4:00
5:00
6:00
7:00
8:00
9:00
10:00

23 Wednesday
READ
1 John 1

6:00
7:00
8:00
9:00
10:00
11:00
12:00
1:00
2:00
3:00
4:00
5:00
6:00
7:00
8:00
9:00
10:00

You're included. I know what it's like to feel on the fringe. To not be invited. To be excluded for reasons you can't control. But when it comes to God's family, I've gone the extra mile to make sure you're a part. Welcome to the family!

Love Jesus

Galatians 3:26-28

24 Thursday

READ
1 John 2

6:00

7:00

8:00

9:00

10:00

11:00

12:00

1:00

2:00

3:00

4:00

5:00

6:00

7:00

8:00

9:00

10:00

25 Friday

READ
1 John 3

6:00

7:00

8:00

9:00

10:00

11:00

12:00

1:00

2:00

3:00

4:00

5:00

6:00

7:00

8:00

9:00

10:00

26 Saturday

READ
1 John 4

6:00

7:00

8:00

9:00

10:00

11:00

12:00

1:00

2:00

3:00

4:00

5:00

6:00

7:00

8:00

9:00

10:00

What are your prayer priorities this week?

To Do

Things you're thankful for this week:

27 Sunday	28 Monday	29 Tuesday	30 Wednesday
READ *1 John 5*	READ *2 John 1*	READ *3 John 1*	READ *Jude 1*
6:00	6:00	6:00	6:00
7:00	7:00	7:00	7:00
8:00	8:00	8:00	8:00
9:00	9:00	9:00	9:00
10:00	10:00	10:00	10:00
11:00	11:00	11:00	11:00
12:00	12:00	12:00	12:00
1:00	1:00	1:00	1:00
2:00	2:00	2:00	2:00
3:00	3:00	3:00	3:00
4:00	4:00	4:00	4:00
5:00	5:00	5:00	5:00
6:00	6:00	6:00	6:00
7:00	7:00	7:00	7:00
8:00	8:00	8:00	8:00
9:00	9:00	9:00	9:00
10:00	10:00	10:00	10:00

You're includers. Remember when I surprised everyone by including kids in my busy schedule? You should have seen the looks on my friends' faces! Now *you* do that, too. You welcome and include others—even the little guys. In doing so, you welcome me. Thanks.

Love, Jesus

Mark 9:37

1 Thursday

READN
Isaiah 7

6:00

7:00

8:00

9:00

10:00

11:00

12:00

1:00

2:00

3:00

4:00

5:00

6:00

7:00

8:00

9:00

10:00

2 Friday

READ
Isaiah 9

6:00

7:00

8:00

9:00

10:00

11:00

12:00

1:00

2:00

3:00

4:00

5:00

6:00

7:00

8:00

9:00

10:00

3 Saturday

READ
Isaiah 11

6:00

7:00

8:00

9:00

10:00

11:00

12:00

1:00

2:00

3:00

4:00

5:00

6:00

7:00

8:00

9:00

10:00

What are your prayer priorities this week?

To Do

Things you're thankful for this week:

Review your gratitude notes from previous weeks, and write a prayer to Jesus thanking him for this month.

What experiences, insights, and moments helped keep Jesus a priority in your life in November? Record them here so you don't forget them.

Reviewing the previous month, how did focusing on the right priorities make a difference in your life?

Are there any ways you might adjust your priorities in the month ahead?

Review your appointments and tasks for the coming month. In what ways are they helping you focus on Jesus' priority of loving others? Is there anything you need to cancel, add, or change? Pray about it; then update your schedule as needed.

Now write a prayer thanking Jesus for new opportunities coming in December, and include one way you're planning to stay focused on him.

To Do

Notes

Sunday	Monday	Tuesday
27	28	29
4	5	6
11	12	13
18	19	20
25 Christmas Day	26	27

This month, keep your priorities focused on Jesus by...

Wednesday	Thursday	Friday	Saturday
30	1	2	3
7	8	9	10
14	15	16	17
21	22	23	24 Christmas Eve
28	29	30	31 New Year's Eve

Loving others: Loving others must always show up in your priorities.
Who are you going to show love to this month? Write one to three names
here, and schedule time to reach out to those people.

4 *Sunday*	*5* *Monday*	*6* *Tuesday*	*7* *Wednesday*
READ	READ	READ	READ
Isaiah 32	*Isaiah 35*	*Isaiah 49*	*Isaiah 54*
6:00	6:00	6:00	6:00
7:00	7:00	7:00	7:00
8:00	8:00	8:00	8:00
9:00	9:00	9:00	9:00
10:00	10:00	10:00	10:00
11:00	11:00	11:00	11:00
12:00	12:00	12:00	12:00
1:00	1:00	1:00	1:00
2:00	2:00	2:00	2:00
3:00	3:00	3:00	3:00
4:00	4:00	4:00	4:00
5:00	5:00	5:00	5:00
6:00	6:00	6:00	6:00
7:00	7:00	7:00	7:00
8:00	8:00	8:00	8:00
9:00	9:00	9:00	9:00
10:00	10:00	10:00	10:00

You're known. Believe me, I can pick you out of a crowd. I know where you are, what you're like, even what you're thinking! I know you better than you know yourself. Don't worry —that's a good thing! As you get to know me more, I'll show you more of who we are together.

Love, Jesus.

John 10:27

8 Thursday

READapproximate
Isaiah 56

6:00

7:00

8:00

9:00

10:00

11:00

12:00

1:00

2:00

3:00

4:00

5:00

6:00

7:00

8:00

9:00

10:00

9 Friday

READ
Isaiah 60

6:00

7:00

8:00

9:00

10:00

11:00

12:00

1:00

2:00

3:00

4:00

5:00

6:00

7:00

8:00

9:00

10:00

10 Saturday

READ
Isaiah 63

6:00

7:00

8:00

9:00

10:00

11:00

12:00

1:00

2:00

3:00

4:00

5:00

6:00

7:00

8:00

9:00

10:00

What are your prayer priorities this week?

To Do

Things you're thankful for this week:

11 Sunday

READ
Isaiah 66

6:00

7:00

8:00

9:00

10:00

11:00

12:00

1:00

2:00

3:00

4:00

5:00

6:00

7:00

8:00

9:00

10:00

12 Monday

READ
Jeremiah 23

6:00

7:00

8:00

9:00

10:00

11:00

12:00

1:00

2:00

3:00

4:00

5:00

6:00

7:00

8:00

9:00

10:00

13 Tuesday

READ
Micah 5

6:00

7:00

8:00

9:00

10:00

11:00

12:00

1:00

2:00

3:00

4:00

5:00

6:00

7:00

8:00

9:00

10:00

14 Wednesday

READ
Zechariah 9

6:00

7:00

8:00

9:00

10:00

11:00

12:00

1:00

2:00

3:00

4:00

5:00

6:00

7:00

8:00

9:00

10:00

You're safe. The world can be a scary place. You'll face death, demons, worry, and fear. But you're in good hands. Nothing can change my love for you. My love has saved you, will protect you, and never, ever stops. You're safe.

Love, Jesus.

Romans 8:38

15 Thursday

READ
Psalm 48

6:00

7:00

8:00

9:00

10:00

11:00

12:00

1:00

2:00

3:00

4:00

5:00

6:00

7:00

8:00

9:00

10:00

16 Friday

READ
Psalm 61

6:00

7:00

8:00

9:00

10:00

11:00

12:00

1:00

2:00

3:00

4:00

5:00

6:00

7:00

8:00

9:00

10:00

17 Saturday

READ
Psalm 67

6:00

7:00

8:00

9:00

10:00

11:00

12:00

1:00

2:00

3:00

4:00

5:00

6:00

7:00

8:00

9:00

10:00

What are your prayer priorities this week?

To Do

Things you're thankful for this week:

18 Sunday

READ
Psalm 70

6:00

7:00

8:00

9:00

10:00

11:00

12:00

1:00

2:00

3:00

4:00

5:00

6:00

7:00

8:00

9:00

10:00

19 Monday

READ
Psalm 82

6:00

7:00

8:00

9:00

10:00

11:00

12:00

1:00

2:00

3:00

4:00

5:00

6:00

7:00

8:00

9:00

10:00

20 Tuesday

READ
Psalm 96

6:00

7:00

8:00

9:00

10:00

11:00

12:00

1:00

2:00

3:00

4:00

5:00

6:00

7:00

8:00

9:00

10:00

21 Wednesday

READ
Matthew 1

6:00

7:00

8:00

9:00

10:00

11:00

12:00

1:00

2:00

3:00

4:00

5:00

6:00

7:00

8:00

9:00

10:00

You're a pattern-breaker. Some patterns are lovely; others not so much. You don't copy the world's ugly behavior. Instead, God has transformed you into a bright fabric of love among repeating patterns of shame. You're different, and it shows—in a good and godly way.

Love, Jesus.

Romans 12:2

22 Thursday

READ
Matthew 2

6:00

7:00

8:00

9:00

10:00

11:00

12:00

1:00

2:00

3:00

4:00

5:00

6:00

7:00

8:00

9:00

10:00

23 Friday

READ
Luke 1:1-38

6:00

7:00

8:00

9:00

10:00

11:00

12:00

1:00

2:00

3:00

4:00

5:00

6:00

7:00

8:00

9:00

10:00

24 Saturday

READ
Luke 1:39-80

6:00

7:00

8:00

9:00

10:00

11:00

12:00

1:00

2:00

3:00

4:00

5:00

6:00

7:00

8:00

9:00

10:00

What are your prayer priorities this week?

To Do

Things you're thankful for this week:

25 Sunday

READ
Luke 2:1-20

6:00	
7:00	
8:00	
9:00	
10:00	
11:00	
12:00	
1:00	
2:00	
3:00	
4:00	
5:00	
6:00	
7:00	
8:00	
9:00	
10:00	

26 Monday

READ
Luke 2:21-51

6:00	
7:00	
8:00	
9:00	
10:00	
11:00	
12:00	
1:00	
2:00	
3:00	
4:00	
5:00	
6:00	
7:00	
8:00	
9:00	
10:00	

27 Tuesday

READ
Galatians 4

6:00	
7:00	
8:00	
9:00	
10:00	
11:00	
12:00	
1:00	
2:00	
3:00	
4:00	
5:00	
6:00	
7:00	
8:00	
9:00	
10:00	

28 Wednesday

READ
Psalm 145

6:00	
7:00	
8:00	
9:00	
10:00	
11:00	
12:00	
1:00	
2:00	
3:00	
4:00	
5:00	
6:00	
7:00	
8:00	
9:00	
10:00	

You're part of the story. The Father knew about you when the world began. Each chapter of his story of Love was written to include you. And the story continues! You're a key figure in redemption's plot each and every day.

Love, Jesus.

Romans 8:29-30

29 Thursday	30 Friday	31 Saturday
READ	READ	
Psalm 146	*Psalm 147*	*Psalm 150*

29 Thursday — READ *Psalm 146*

6:00
7:00
8:00
9:00
10:00
11:00
12:00
1:00
2:00
3:00
4:00
5:00
6:00
7:00
8:00
9:00
10:00

30 Friday — READ *Psalm 147*

6:00
7:00
8:00
9:00
10:00
11:00
12:00
1:00
2:00
3:00
4:00
5:00
6:00
7:00
8:00
9:00
10:00

31 Saturday — *Psalm 150*

6:00
7:00
8:00
9:00
10:00
11:00
12:00
1:00
2:00
3:00
4:00
5:00
6:00
7:00
8:00
9:00
10:00

What are your prayer priorities this week?

To Do

Things you're thankful for this week:

Review your gratitude notes from previous weeks, and write a prayer to Jesus thanking him for this month.

What experiences, insights, and moments helped keep Jesus a priority in your life in December? Record them here so you don't forget them.

Reviewing the previous month, how did focusing on the right priorities make a difference in your life?

Are there any ways you might adjust your priorities in the month ahead?

Review your appointments and tasks for the coming month. In what ways are they helping you focus on Jesus' priority of loving others? Is there anything you need to cancel, add, or change? Pray about it; then update your schedule as needed.

Now write a prayer thanking Jesus for new opportunities coming in the new year, and include one way you're planning to stay focused on him.